HAUNTED HEART OF LOS ANGELES

BRIAN CLUNE

WITH PHOTOGRAPHY BY TERRI CLUNE

Published by Haunted America
A Division of The History Press
Charleston, SC
www.historypress.com

Unless otherwise noted, all photos are courtesy of Terri Clune.

First published 2024

Manufactured in the United States

ISBN 9781467157797

Library of Congress Control Number: 2024938199

Notice: The information in this book is true and complete to the best of our knowledge. It is offered without guarantee on the part of the author or The History Press. The author and The History Press disclaim all liability in connection with the use of this book.

Having started as a small pueblo, Los Angeles is now the largest city in California.

This book is dedicated to my wife, Terri, for her steadfast determination to never let me deviate from my subject matter and for taking some really good photos.

I also dedicate this book to my buddy Bob Davis. He has gone through so much lately in his personal life but has weathered the storm with dignity, grace and strength.

I love you both!

Tip the world over on its side and everything loose will land in Los Angeles.

—Frank Lloyd Wright

CONTENTS

Acknowledgements

So many folks are needed to complete one small book, not just the author but all of those who support the author as well. With this in mind, I would like to thank all of those who dedicate their lives to keeping the wonderful history of Los Angeles alive. It is not always easy, and these folks work tirelessly to keep ancient buildings from crumbling to the ground and historic monuments from being erased from memory and make sure that the history of Los Angeles is preserved for future generations—and for authors like me who like to write about these locations.

As always, I must thank Laurie Krill, my acquisitions editor, for constantly answering my calls and laughing at me every time I come up with another book idea yet always having my back when things may not go my way. Thank you, Laurie.

I also want to thank Joe Gorman for always helping me get the books I need for events, signings and other appearances I may have. You're the best, Joe.

INTRODUCTION

THE CITY OF ANGELS

Los Angeles, the City of Angels: folks flock here from all over the world to see the great city where Hollywood shines, history abounds and stars and starlets wait around every corner. Los Angeles—known for its authentic Mexican cuisine, Philippe the Original (creator of the French Dip sandwich) and historic Cinco de Mayo celebrations—has earned a reputation around the globe as a cosmopolitan metropolis to rival New York, Chicago and San Francisco as one of the most visited cities in the country. Many know about the riots that occurred in 1965 and again in 1992 and how they helped shape the civil rights movements that are still, we hope, advancing to this day. From the violence of those events to the 1871 lynching of seventeen Chinese immigrants in Chinatown and the forced, deadly relocation of the residents of Chavez Ravine so a major league baseball team could move to the West Coast, Los Angeles has seen its fair share of heartache and treachery.

From its humble beginnings in the late 1700s, Los Angeles grew rapidly and, like every city in the nation, had its own unique growing pains and problems. Despite four separate peoples claiming ownership of the land and three powerful countries controlling and claiming ownership in the short span of under one hundred years, LA would weather all tribulations and become the gem of Southern California. But as history shows us again and again, growth can be tumultuous and cruel, deadly and violent. Growth can cause the veil between worlds to rip and tear and bring forth things that would be best left in the dimensions beyond our own. In that regard, Los Angeles is no different than any other city.

Angels Flight, in Los Angeles, the world's shortest railway, was built in 1901 and is known to be haunted by a man who was killed on the funicular.

From lands cursed by a greedy Spaniard to the lynching of innocent people and criminals alike and the deaths of residents just trying to live their lives after the many earthquakes that have ravaged the city, Los Angeles has known the darker side of life. With its riots and growing gang influence, mixed with serial killers and famous unsolved murders, Los Angeles is also no stranger to the evil side of mankind. Suicides, traffic accidents and natural deaths all come together in big cities across the United States, and the City of Angels is no different in that regard, but what makes LA unusual is the diversity of peoples who have laid claim to this area for hundreds and even thousands of years. Alongside all this diversity come the hardships and misery of growth in the big city.

With everything that Los Angeles has had to endure—not only the city but also her people—it should come as no surprise that Los Angeles may be the most haunted city in California, maybe even the entire West Coast. With this in mind, sit back in a comfortable chair or under the covers of your nice, safe bed, and get ready to read some truly terrifying tales of ghosts, legends and cursed lands in a town known as the City of Angels. But fear not, for every story you are about to read is said to be real.

CHAPTER 1

LOS ANGELES: ITS COLORFUL HISTORY

Los Angeles, like so many other cities in California, has humble roots. Also, like most of the towns and pueblos of Alta California, its beginnings came at a cost for the Natives who were already living there. Now the second largest city in the United States and the biggest economic center on the West Coast, it was originally the home of the Chumash, Tongva and other Native tribes since about 8000 BC. When Portuguese captain Juan Rodriguez Cabrillo began exploring the area in 1542, he found the Natives to be receptive but wary of the newcomers. After this first European expedition departed, it would be more than two hundred years before Gaspar de Portolá would establish a Spanish outpost in what we now recognize as the Los Angeles Basin.

In 1769, Gaspar de Portolá, on orders from the Spanish governor in Mexico, set up a small outpost in the Native village near what is today the Los Angeles River. His expedition was tasked with helping Padre Junipero Serra set up a series of missions, each a day's walk from the next, as a way to bring the word of Christianity to the Natives and identify locations where presidios (forts) might be needed to protect Spanish interests while colonizing Alta California. The outpost grew larger when, in 1781, Spanish governor Filipe de Neve sent *pobladores* to begin colonizing the area. These forty-four *pobladores* (settlers), fourteen families in all, had a mix of European, Native American and African heritage. Once settled into their pueblo along the river, the residents began farming the land, raising cattle and trading with the Native Chumash and Tongva peoples. Governor de Neve named

From a hill in Los Angeles, one can see the beauty of the surrounding area and why early settlers chose to live here.

the new settlement El Pueblo de Nuestra Señora la Reina de Los Ángeles de Porciúncula, or the Town of Our Lady the Queen of the Angels of Porciúncula. Over time, the name of the pueblo became simply Los Angeles.

As the mission system grew, so did the pueblo. First came the Mission San Gabriel Arcángel, followed by Mission San Fernando (named in honor of Ferdinand III of Spain), and with Los Angles being between the two and surrounded by fertile soil and the plentiful waters of the river, its population grew fairly quickly. As with most pueblos and towns of the time, residents congregated around a central plaza. Here, the townsfolk would hold meetings, celebrations, weddings and funerals, and Los Angeles was no different. At first, the Natives traded and worked with and for the residents of the pueblo, but over time, the two parties began to grow distant. With the Spanish mistreating Natives in and around the missions by forcing them to convert and treating many as slaves, trust of the Spaniards was waning rapidly among the Native people. After uprisings at Mission San Gabriel and Mission La Purisima, the Chumash, Tongva and others began to shy away from the folks in the pueblo. Then, as the end of the century came, the Mexicans, including those of Spanish descent, began to question the rule of a government so far away on another continent and the way in which it was treating the Mexican people.

By 1810, many Mexicans had had enough of Spanish governance of Mexico. On September 16, 1810, Miguel Hidalgo y Costilla, a Catholic priest, rallied Mexicans everywhere with the Grito de Dolores, or Cry of Dolores (so called due to Hidalgo publicly reading the revolutionary plea in the pueblo of Dolores) calling for the end of Spanish rule in Mexico. Thousands of mestizos (persons of mixed blood), Natives and peasants rose to Hidalgo's Virgin of Guadalupe banner and marched on Mexico City. Hidalgo, although close to capturing the capital city, was defeated and driven back and eventually had to flee after the peasant army was again bested at Calderón. Hidalgo was finally captured and executed in 1811. Although he was put to death, his sacrifice led to others picking up his torch, and one after the other, they harried the Spanish forces until 1821, when Spain ceded to the Mexican forces and Mexico gained its independence.

Not much changed for the pueblo of Los Angeles either during or after the Mexican War of Independence: life simply went on. The one change that was noticed was the lack of interest Mexico had in the goings-on of its northern territories. Mexico was struggling to find its footing, from naming a new emperor to figuring out how to best support its outlying holdings while trying to maintain a modicum of available finances, and Alta California, while not ignored, was considered secondary to Mexico itself. Needless to say, the citizens of Alta California were not happy about the situation. As the United States still practiced "manifest destiny" and expansion, the Mexican American War broke out, and many in Alta California openly backed the United States in the conflict. Many believed that if Washington won the war, their lot in life would drastically improve. In 1848, after the Treaty of Guadalupe Hidalgo was signed and the United States paid $15 million for 55 percent of Mexico's territory, the Pueblo of Los Angeles had its wish: it was now part of the United States—and not a moment too soon. Just after the war ended, rich gold veins were discovered near Sacramento, bringing thousands of prospectors, ranchers, storekeepers and suppliers to California, and many of these depended on the ranches and farms of sunny Los Angeles. The small pueblo at the foot of the mountains was about to see its first big migration.

With thousands of folks flocking to California on their way to the gold fields in the north of the state, many found that riches could be found not in panning for gold or digging through mountainsides but in supplying those who were going to be doing just that. Los Angeles became a stopping point for many coming from the East, along with those who first came in through San Diego on their way to the Sacramento area. These folks needed to be supplied, and shops sprang up to fill this need. After the initial furor of gold fever subsided and the influx of forty-niners slowed down, many of these shopkeepers decided to stay. The beautiful Southern California climate, weather and scenery were the main draw; however, folks also came to realize that Los Angeles was growing, and they wanted to be a part of it. When, in 1881, the Southern Pacific Railroad completed a track into Los Angeles, even more Easterners came looking for the promised orange groves, beaches and everlasting sunshine. Land was being sold to anyone and everyone who could afford it, and the plentiful water that had been available began to disappear at an alarming rate. Enter William Mullholland.

Knowing that both people and farm crops needed water to survive and that without it, Los Angeles could never grow or sustain its pace of rising prominence, Mullholland knew that he had to do something to bring more water to the LA basin, so he turned his sights on the water-rich Owens Valley and its river. Using aggressive buying tactics, including backroom deals, trickery, bribery and downright illegal means, Mullholland acquired almost all land and water rights to the lush valley north of Los Angeles. It took him a while to gain the rights, but in September 1907, construction began on a roughly two-hundred-mile aqueduct that would slake the thirst of the

A short distance outside LA proper, Hollywood draws folks from all over the world to Los Angeles.

citizens of Los Angeles but would turn the lush, green Owens Valley into a desert and Owens Lake, once one of the largest inland bodies of water in the United States, into nothing more than a dust-filled crater with a creek running through it. On November 5, 1913, when the aqueduct opened, Los Angeles had its water—but at what cost? Mullholland told forty thousand smiling Angelinos, "There it is, take it!" That one statement sums up his attitude perfectly.

Shortly after Los Angeles began using its stolen water, film scouts began coming to LA. Most studios were headquartered in the northeastern United States, and scouts were looking for areas that would allow a long filming season, where more sunshine, less rain and a whole lot less snow would support production. Small studios began to pop up all over LA, especially in and around the area known as Village Hollywood. In 1914, when Cecil B. DeMille filmed *The Squaw Man*, it put Los Angeles on the map for every film entrepreneur in the country, and then, in 1915, when Carl Laemmle opened his Universal City, there was no turning back: the Hollywood area of LA would forever be known as the birthplace of movies. After World War I, almost every studio in the country followed Universal, which had the added effect of bringing many "star hopefuls" out to LA, and even though most

The Brunswig Building, across the street from the plaza, is one of the oldest buildings in LA and rumored to be haunted.

didn't make it big in Hollywood, they stayed in Los Angeles for the beautiful weather and sunshine. Then, after World War II, with many soldiers who had served in the Pacific Theater being repatriated through California, thousands of U.S. service personnel decided to call LA home. Los Angeles was now considered a world-class city, and there was no stopping her now.

From its humble beginnings through its tumultuous growth, wars and changes of government, Los Angeles has endured. Riots, race wars, earthquakes and other natural catastrophes tried in vain to bring the city down, but she survived. Corrupt politicians, a destructive national baseball scandal as well as theft of life-sustaining water rights tried and failed, but Los Angeles has weathered them all and more. Through everything, Los Angeles has remained true to her Spanish and Mexican roots, and Angelinos have kept those roots alive through culture and remembrance of who they truly are. All one needs to do is visit Olvera Street and El Pueblo de Los Angeles to understand the depth of feeling her citizens have for the City of Angels.

CHAPTER 2

EL PUEBLO DE LOS ANGELES (OLVERA STREET)

If Griffith Park is the heart of the city, then El Pueblo de Los Angeles and the surrounding area is the lifeblood that keeps its history alive. It was here that the City of Los Angeles began and where the first plaza was built so the families of early Los Angeles could gather for their meetings, celebrations, funerals and weddings. It was here that the last Mexican governor of California built his home and hotel, and it is here that the oldest adobe in the city still sits; the plaza is also where LA's first church, firehouse and theater were built. Olvera Street, as the area is named, has seen riots, lynch mobs and countless school field trip groups pass through its lanes, and the history it has seen is an education in and of itself. Despite almost falling to a developer's wrecking ball, El Pueblo de Los Angeles, through it all, has survived. Still mired in racial controversy to this day, Olvera Street has become a tourist attraction and history time capsule for all those who have come to live in the City of Angels.

Olvera Street is the oldest part of Downtown Los Angeles, and although many folks call this the birthplace of the city, it is actually where the city moved after unpredictable flooding kept soaking the original pueblo. The birthplace of LA is certainly close (approximately two blocks north of Olvera Street along the LA River), just not at Olvera Street. El Pueblo de Los Angeles was established here in the early 1800s, and the area grew, with a cattle, farming and wine-producing economy. Even today, there are still vineyards producing fine wines using grapes that originated at the Mission San Gabriel sometime around 1771 (DNA samples have confirmed this).

The rotunda, in the middle of the plaza on Olvera Street, sits where the original citizens would gather for festivities and meetings.

Because of these vineyards, Olvera Street's original name was either Wine Street or Vine Street, depending on which map one looks at. There is a slight bit of controversy about the name, with some claiming "Vine" only appeared on one of the original maps because the word *wine* had been spilled on, "erasing half of the 'W' in the word 'Wine'"; we may never have a definitive answer to this, but feel free to come to your own conclusion. In 1877, Wine/Vine Street was officially renamed Olvera Street (it was actually more of an alley) in honor of the county's first judge, Agustín Olvera.

Immigrants from Mexico still migrated to Los Angeles, but as the city grew, so did its diversity. The U.S. Civil War brought folks from back east and the South, many with differing viewpoints on the merits of the war. Due to rising favorable sentiment toward the Southern states, Lincoln established forts up and down the coast of California, one of the largest being Fort Drum, a short distance from Los Angeles. This brought not only soldiers to man the forts but also traders to feed, clothe and outfit them and folks to work on the docks that received the needed goods. A large number of Chinese nationals also came to work on the railroads that were being built up and down the state, along with those tracks being laid from the lines coming from the east. Even after the war, this diverse population stayed due to the weather and opportunities that the area had to offer.

By 1871, the population of Los Angeles was approaching 6,000; of that, the U.S. Census noted, 172 were Chinese, roughly 3 percent of the total population of 5,728. A majority of the Chinese lived in adobes along Calle de los Negros, or Negro Alley (so named for the dark-skinned Spaniards who originally populated this area). Today, this area is part of Union Station across from Olvera Street and the plaza. This section of the city was the "vice district" of Los Angeles, with brothels, gambling halls and more saloons than one could count lining the unpaved alley. The area was dirty and violent and had the distinction of the highest murder rate in the nation. Add to this that Los Angeles employed only six police officers, and one can see why LA was such a crime-ridden place. Lynchings, shootings and mob justice were the norm rather than the exception. However vicious the area had become, the violence was rarely race based, and few attacks against the Chinese population occurred. That all changed in 1871, when the *Los Angeles News* and the *Los Angeles Star* began condemning the Chinese as "immoral" and "inferior." Given these editorials and the anger over Chinese immigration they provoked, it isn't surprising that racial attacks against the Chinese population began. This hatred would all come to a violent head on October 24, 1871.

"Mexican quarter of Los Angeles, California. Average rental eight dollars. Some houses have plumbing." *New York Public Library Digital Collections.*

In October 1871, Chinatown was embroiled in a feud between two rival *huiguan* (mutual benefit associations) over the kidnapping of a Chinese woman that had occurred in San Francisco, which spilled over into Los Angeles. This kidnapping caused a shootout to take place between several Chinese men in Negro Alley. Two officers responded with the help of a civilian named Robert Thompson. The Chinese antagonists either didn't hear the officers demand that they surrender or, more likely, didn't care and ended up wounding one officer and killing Thompson. The Chinese then retreated to the Coronel Adobe and barricaded themselves inside. It wasn't long before word spread that Thompson, a well-liked former saloon owner, had been gunned down and killed, and a mob formed lusting for Chinese blood. Soon, five hundred rioters, almost 10 percent of the population, had stormed the Coronel, forcing every Chinese man out of the building, dragging them to a makeshift gallows at nearby Tomlinson's corral and hanging them. Out of room for more lynchings on the crosspiece at the corral, they moved to Goller's wagon shop to finish their grisly work. However, when John Goller tried to stop them because his children were watching, one of the rioters pressed a gun to his face and told him, "Dry up, you son of a bitch." Now, with seven Chinese men hanging from Goller's portico crossbar, the rioters dragged the last three to a freight wagon and hanged them from the high sides of the wagon itself. This was the worst mass murder in the history of Los Angeles.

One of the most reprehensible things about mob rule is that it can take on a mind and will of its own. During this night of savagery, one woman was heard yelling from her nearby shop, "Hang them all!" This precipitated her young son joining the gruesome event. One of the victims of the lynching was completely innocent of any offense; that person was Dr. Gene Tong. Tong was one of the most respected citizens of the area, known and liked by everyone: White, Chinese, Mexican and all others of the diversified city. Tong had an office in the Coronel Adobe and was unfortunately there when the violence began. It is said that as he was being dragged away by the unreasoning and uncivilized mob, Dr. Tong tried to profess his innocence, but instead of listening to him, one of the mindless group shot his jaw off to keep him silent. It is also said that as he hung there, still alive, someone in the group cut off his finger to steal his wedding ring. Dr. Tong is a sad example of what mob mentality produces: of the eighteen men and boys brutally lynched that night, it is said that only one was from the group of Chinese who had started the situation.

As the end of the 1800s approached, Los Angeles was expanding rapidly. As such, the downtown area was being overlooked as attention was focused

Looking out from the courtyard of the Avila Adobe, on Olvera Street, one can see how close Union Station, once Chinatown, is to the plaza.

outward on other areas surrounding Olvera Street, and this area became the most overlooked of them all. The historic adobes began to crumble and fall. Where Chinatown stood across the street from the plaza wasn't much better, and poverty reigned supreme. Because of this, Olvera Street was all but forgotten. What was once the heart of Mexican culture in Los Angeles, due to its decline, became a beacon for the poor and a draw for those radicals fomenting revolution within the United States. Anarchist Emma Goldman used the backdrop of the crumbling plaza to spread her radical politics, and the father of modern China, Sun Yat-sen, spoke here, spreading his revolutionary ideas to the United States. All this aside, the poverty continued and so did the decline and neglect of the "birthplace" of Los Angeles. Here is where Christine Sterling stepped in to become known as the Mother of Olvera Street.

Born Chastina Rix in chilly Northern California in 1881 to a scientist father and a grandfather who was an important San Francisco judge, Rix may not have been born with a silver spoon in her mouth, but her family certainly wasn't poor. Growing up, Rix read all she could about the Wild West, and after reading Helen Hunt Jackson's book *Ramona*, she fell in love with Native American culture and, even more so, with the Mexican way of life and traditions. She couldn't read enough about the people of Mexico, gathering booklets and other source material about Los Angeles and Mexican romance. Chastina Rix dreamed of coming to LA and wrote about it extensively in her journals: "They were appealing with old missions, palm trees, sunshine and the click of castanets."

Having changed her name to Christine as a teenager, Rix attended school at Mills College, studying art. After her first marriage failed, Christine married attorney Jerome Hough and gave birth to two children, June and Peter. The couple eventually moved to Los Angeles, much to Christine's delight, and lived on Bonnie Brae Street very close to downtown. After moving to the city of her dreams, Christine found in it disappointment, writing, "At last Los Angeles was home. The sunshine, mountains, beaches, palm trees were here, but where was the romance of the past?" Not only did the city seem to let her down, but it also wasn't long before her husband up and left without saying a word. After his departure, Christine once again changed her name to reinvent herself, and the name Christine Sterling would forever become a part of Los Angeles lore.

Sometime in 1926, Sterling headed out for a walk through downtown, seeking the Los Angeles she had always dreamed about. "I visited the old plaza, the birthplace of the city and found it forsaken and forgotten. Down a dirty alley, I discovered an old adobe, dignified even in its decay. Across the front door was nailed a black and white sign, 'CONDEMNED.'" This one

Casa Avila. *Historic American Buildings Survey, via Library of Congress.*

sign, attached to the front door of the Avila Adobe, would set into motion one woman's need to bring back the Los Angeles of old, her dream of a romantic Mexican marketplace and the refurbishment of a downtown in decline, even if it wasn't historically accurate.

The "dirty alley" Sterling had wandered down was Olvera Street, and the adobe was the fabled building that was and is the oldest structure in—and was once the social center of—LA. Seeing the once-handsome adobe, Sterling knew she had to save not only the building but also the area surrounding it. She set out to bring awareness to the plight of the old downtown and began a fundraising campaign to begin restoration. Petitioning city leaders by reminding them that LA was home to two hundred thousand Mexicans, she stood before them and said, "It might be well to take our Mexican population seriously and allow them to put a little romance and picturesque into our city which we so freely advertise ourselves as possessing. The plaza should be converted into a social and commercial Latin American center." It wasn't until Sterling had convinced *Los Angeles Times* president Harry Chandler, the most powerful man in Los Angeles, to support her vague idea of a marketplace that the rest of the city, including the politicians, jumped onboard as well.

Once Chandler became involved, it was all but impossible for the city's elite to stay out of the restoration. When Harry Chandler invited you to a "luncheon" or "dinner," you made sure to attend, and you made sure you had your checkbook with you. After Chandler held a fundraising lunch on the patio of the Avila Adobe, the money and donations began coming in for the restoration of Olvera Street. Even local law enforcement joined in by sending incarcerated felons to be used as laborers. In her journal, Sterling wrote, "With my two children, 25 prisoners, 50% protest from property owners and a lawsuit thrown in for good measure, we put the first picks and shovels into the old street. The prisoners were good workers, one escaped, but we managed to keep the others." She went on to admit, "One of the prisoners is a good carpenter, another an electrician. Each night I pray they will arrest a bricklayer and a plumber." In a strange twist of fate, only two days after Sterling admitted her wish, two bricklayers were arrested. Unfortunately, no plumber decided to break the law.

The reason for the protest and lawsuit was, in no small part, the false narrative and inaccurate vision of what a Mexican marketplace would look like from a historical perspective. While trying to get funding and support, Christine Sterling emphasized the history of the adobe in the United States over its true Mexican roots. Writer and historian William Estrada explained

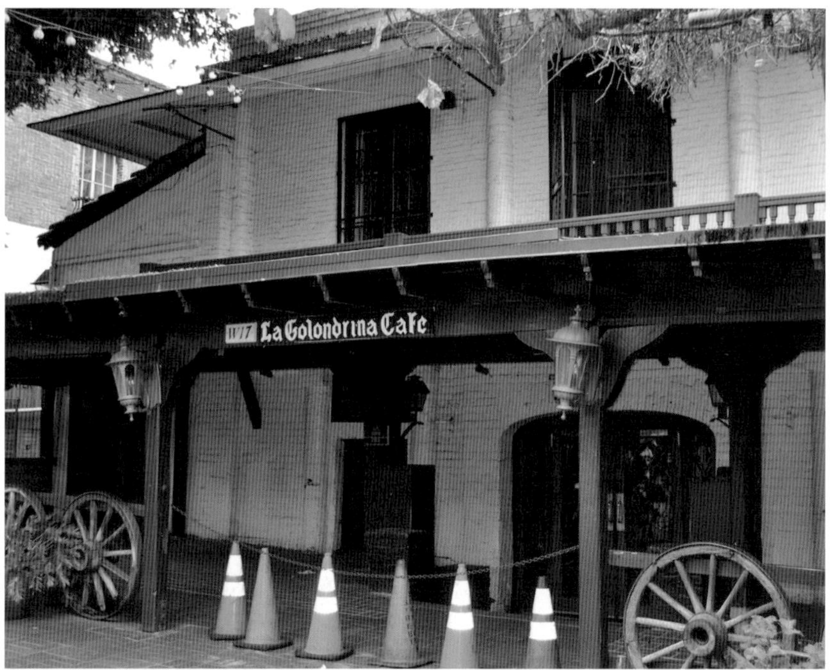

La Golondrina is the oldest restaurant in LA. Unfortunately, it is now closed due to issues with the city. It is not known if it will ever reopen. It is said to be haunted by the original owners and past residents of Olvera Street.

Today, Olvera Street is a tourist stop selling both real and faux Mexican trinkets. The entirety of this little street is said to have a lot of haunting activity.

Hispanic communities have always been religious, and this reverence is still prevalent today.

it in a *Los Angeles Times* piece in 2005 this way: "Appealing to an Anglo audience, she conjured up Anglo heroes [in the same way as]…'George Washington slept here'—not the fact that Francisco Avila built this adobe and was a rancher and one time mayor of the city." Although her tactic worked, many say that it revealed her complete disregard for actual history and her romanticized vision of the past, which made Olvera Street nothing more than the tourist attraction it is now. Regardless of the controversy, which is still going on even to this day, Olvera Street opened to the public on Easter Sunday, April 30, 1930, as Paseo de Los Angeles, now popularly known as Olvera Street.

After Christine Sterling was finished "saving" Olvera Street, she turned her attention to doing the same for Chinatown. After Paseo de Los Angeles opened, the push for a union train station to replace the three depots already in downtown LA grew to a fever pitch. It wasn't long before the removal of the Chinese from Chinatown to make way for the train station —already in legal dispute after a controversial ballot measure approved by voters in 1926—was approved. Sterling believed that she had the answer with her "China City" project, but unlike Olvera Street's Hispanics, the Chinese were not onboard in the least with her vision of what a Chinese neighborhood should look like. Chinatown was moved after Union Station was approved, and even though Sterling did build her fantasy version of China, it mysteriously caught fire and burned to the ground, never to be rebuilt.

In what some call a twist of fate and others call fate's retribution, Christine Sterling was forcibly removed from her home in Chaves Ravine to make way for Dodger Stadium. She had to move into a small apartment in the Avila Adobe, where she stayed until she passed away in the summer of 1963. Say what you will about Olvera Street, fantasy or history, but one thing is for sure: many, if not most of those working and owning the shops and stalls there today are the same Mexican families who have been there for generations and who plan to stay there as long as Olvera Street remains in existence. Most love and respect what Christine Sterling gave them and Los Angeles. Others, of course, cannot or will never approve of the Paseo de Los Angeles or what it was meant to portray, even if it was a romanticized vision of Mexico. As William Estrada told the *Los Angeles Times*, "Olvera Street is an imagined space, an invented space. There are a lot of innocent interpretations. I've heard, 'This is the oldest street in L.A.' or 'This is what L.A. looked like 200 years ago.' Olvera Street was created in 1930 by an Anglo woman, Christine Sterling who wanted to create a Mexican marketplace."

New Chinatown, although not where Sterling had wanted it, became one of the premier Chinatowns in the world thanks to its Chinese citizenry.

I will leave it to you, the reader, to decide what to make of this downtown tourist attraction. However, with all the turmoil this small alley has seen over the years it's been around and all the life, death and murder the area has witnessed, it should come as no surprise that many of the buildings, restaurants and walkways are known to be haunted by those who once called the area home.

CHAPTER 3

AVILA ADOBE

The Avila Adobe, which sits at the north end of Olvera Street, is the oldest structure in the city of Los Angeles. Built in 1818 by Francisco Avila, the adobe became the centerpiece of the early community and a place that residents came to know well. Over the years, as the area became less and less central to the city, Olvera Street and the adobe along with it began to decline until both were all but forgotten relics of a time long past. The adobe today has been refurbished and stands as a symbol of Spanish and Mexican life in early Los Angeles and the fortitude of those folks to survive when others might fall. It is also a symbol of how humans can remain after death to watch over those things they love, for you see, the Avila Adobe is one of the most haunted places in old LA.

Francisco Avila was born in El Fuerte, New Spain, what is today Sinaloa, Mexico. Avila came to Los Angeles sometime after 1794 (the exact date has been lost) and became deeply involved with the community. By 1810, Francisco had become alcalde (mayor) of Los Angeles. By this time, the population of LA had grown to 415, and Francisco wanted to make sure the residents were well taken care of. In 1823, Mexico, having won independence from Spain, granted Avila 4,439 acres of land as a reward for services to Mexico, and this became the Rancho Las Ciénegas. With the need to run his new holdings, Avila began spending his weeks out at the rancho and would stay at his adobe only on weekends. While at the adobe, Francisco would entertain and hold business meetings and spend as much time as possible with his family. He would also spend holidays at his adobe

It was on this adobe that Sterling saw the letter of condemnation and decided to save Olvera Street for future generations. The Avila Adobe stands to this day.

and hold community events there throughout the year for various festivals. Francisco Avila would become one of the wealthiest Californio ranchers in LA history.

The adobe itself was built in 1818, five years before Avila was given his land grant. As mayor, Avila was a man of some power and means, and to reflect that, he built his adobe to match his stature in the community. Much larger than what we see today, the original structure was an L-shaped building, traditional for the time, with a compacted dirt floor that had to be swept at least twice a day, ceilings that were fifteen feet high and a roof that was sealed with tar from the nearby La Brea Tar Pits, mixed with aggregate and horsehair as a water sealant. Wood floors would be added later which made cleaning the adobe much easier. The home was built of adobe bricks that were almost three feet thick, with a ceiling supported by cottonwood beams hewn from the trees that grew by the Los Angeles River. With several bedrooms, the adobe also included a family room, a living room, an office, a kitchen (the cooking was actually done outside), a patio with a long porch overlooking it, a vineyard and a garden (Francisco loved working in the garden). It has been said that Avila furnished the adobe with imports from Europe and Asia, many brought in by ship from Boston around Cape Horn.

Francisco Avila's first wife, Maria del Rosario Verdugo, passed away in 1822, and her death hit Francisco hard. However, it wasn't long before he took a second wife, Maria Encarnación Sepúlveda, daughter of Francisco Sepúlveda, owner of nearby Rancho Vicente y Santa Mónica. Maria Encarnación loved her husband dearly, and when Francisco passed away in 1832, she was devastated. It is said that she never got over her husband's death and mourned him until the day she died in 1855 and perhaps longer than that. After his death, Maria Encarnación ran the rancho as best she could with the help of his four children. In 1871, the U.S. government recognized and granted Januario Avila, Pedro Avila de Ramirez, Francisca Avila de Rimpau and Louisa Avila de Garfias, Francisco's four children, the rights to Rancho Las Ciénegas.

During the Mexican American war, the Avila Adobe, in 1847, became the temporary headquarters for Commodore Robert F. Stockton and also housed U.S. troops. Through this time, Avila's youngest daughter lived in her family's home, until her death in 1868. This period in the adobe's history is an important intersection, according to an adobe tour guide by the name of Angeliz, who told USC's Annenberg Media in December 2015, "When there was the Mexican American war, this was actually one of the Americans, one of their headquarters for a while, so it's very significant because it's not only Mexican but it's also American." After the war ended and California became a state, the area that was once the center of life in Los Angeles began to wane. Avila family members occupied the adobe over the next few years until it became a boardinghouse; however, after sustaining damage in an 1870 earthquake, the structure began to deteriorate. It seems that during the slow decline of the "Mexican" area of the city, the Avila Adobe followed the same trajectory.

By 1928, the Avila Adobe had become so worn down by time and neglect that the city had no choice but to condemn the structure. Calls for its restoration landed on deaf ears, with many saying that since the entire Pueblo District was now so decrepit, it would be like throwing good money after bad. The city agreed, and the condemnation was decreed. It was at this time that Christine Sterling came across Olvera Street and the sign posted on the door of the Avila Adobe. Without her tireless efforts to save the area and the historic adobe, the city, like so many other cities have done, would have let its history simply fade away under the wrecking ball of time. According to Angeliz, "In 1930, Christine Sterling—the one who made up Olvera Street—because of her we have the Avila Adobe. She was the one that actually saved it because it was about to get demolished.

Because of her they ended up stopping it and then ended up making it a museum."

The history the adobe has seen is remarkable, and it is in fact a part of history itself. It is also a treasure that we should all be grateful was saved by a woman who had a dream, even if it was a vision not based in true-to-life aspects. The adobe itself, even today, can teach us things that history may have forgotten in its race to the future—not its walls, ceilings and furnishings but the fact that those who lived through that history are said to still be present in the adobe to this day. It is said, by those who work there and have visited the museum, that the Avila Adobe is haunted by those who lived, died and loved in the old pueblo.

There are many reasons why a person may remain in a place after death: severe trauma, unfinished business, because it was a place that made them happy or simply because their love of the location makes them want to stay where their life had meaning. It is not uncommon for a location to have spirits that fall into one or two of these categories, but it's rare that a location has them all, like we seem to see at the Avila Adobe.

This may be the bedroom where Christine Sterling passed away, as her spirit has been seen here often.

Francisco Avila built the adobe for himself and his family, and even though after receiving his land grant he spent more time away from home, he was happiest when he was with his family and tending his garden. Over the years, even as the adobe began to crumble, folks would say that they could hear someone tending the garden in the back of the house. They would hear dirt being shoveled, water being "poured from a container" and the telltale sound of a man coughing and taking long, loud breaths and even, on occasion, the sharp grunt or growl of a man at work. Those folks brave enough to venture back to have a look would find nothing but the overgrown weeds and plants of a patio garden unattended for years. Many believe that the spirit heard in the garden is that of Francisco still tending his adobe and enjoying his time in the garden like he did in life.

The former alcalde is also believed to roam within the walls of the adobe as well. Since it has been open as a museum, many guests have reported hearing footsteps walking the halls of the Avila Adobe. Both the sound of heavy boots and shoes described as high heels have been heard pacing up and down the wooden floors. The sound of the boots is thought to be Francisco Avila walking around, looking over his home. One wonders, since the adobe is so much smaller now than in Francisco's day, if he is curious about what happened to the home he built. The sound of footsteps is not the only reason folks are convinced that Avila has stayed at the adobe. There have been many reports about seeing him both inside and outside the old adobe. There have also been reports of people seeing Mayor Avila walking out in front of the home along Olvera Street.

Francisco may be wondering about his home, but others believe he knows full well what transpired to shrink the old adobe and has made his displeasure fully known. A blog post written by cryptic79 tells the story of a group of construction workers who may have had an encounter with an angry Francisco Avila. The construction workers were in the process of restoring sections of the adobe one evening when they broke for lunch. Sitting outside, enjoying the cool evening air, they heard what sounded like heavy furniture being moved inside the adobe. One of the workers checked but could find nothing amiss and had just sat back down with his colleagues when again they heard the sound. This time, however, it sounded as if someone was sliding and crashing furniture from room to room. They all got up, peered into the Avila Adobe and called out to whoever was angrily moving the furniture about. All the sound stopped as they stepped inside, and they found that nothing had been disturbed: everything was in the same place it had been when they began their break.

Francisco Avila himself and other spirits have been seen in the courtyard of the Avila Adobe.

The entire crew decided that no more work needed to be done on the adobe that evening.

As mentioned earlier, Francisco's second wife, Maria Encarnción, was overcome with sorrow when her husband died, and that sorrow lasted for the rest of her life and, it seems, even into her afterlife. Guests touring the Avila Adobe museum have reported hearing mournful sobbing coming from what was the master bedroom. Before her death in 1855, it was said that Maria Encarnción would suddenly stop whatever she was doing, go to the bedroom and cry for her lost husband; she would always come back a few minutes later and finish the task at hand. It is believed that the crying coming from the bedroom may be a residual haunting brought on by the extreme sorrow of a woman who is missing the man she loves. Many believe that they have seen Maria Encarnción sitting on the front porch of the adobe, slowly rocking back and forth, seemingly at peace. We can only hope that this spirit is content and that she and Francisco have been reunited in death and are enjoying a long, happy afterlife together.

Christine Sterling, the woman who brought Olvera Street back to life and gave Los Angeles' Mexican history a voice, ran into trouble after her success with Olvera Street and her failure with China City. After her husband left her and his kids, Sterling moved to Chaves Ravine and was happy being close to the area of the city she loved. Caught up in the Battle of Chaves Ravine which made Major League Baseball's forced relocation of LA's Mexican neighborhood a reality, Sterling and the Mexicans of the area were forced to give up their homes. Some say that it was cosmic justice that forced Sterling to lose her home due to her fantasy version of Mexico, but whatever one wants to believe, Sterling moved into the Avila Adobe and spent the rest of her life in a small apartment in the adobe she all but singlehandedly saved.

Although Sterling did have a somewhat romanticized image of Mexico, she truly loved the Mexican people, their culture and the Avila Adobe. After her death in 1963 (she died in bed at the adobe, and her ashes are still there), many folks began hearing the sound of high heels walking along the halls of the home. During the last renovations of the Avila Adobe from 1971 to 1977, many of the workers would report having the feeling of being constantly watched while performing their work, with a few quitting due to the feeling that someone was looking over their shoulder (they reported feeling someone literally breathing down their necks). Families who have worked the shops along Olvera Street for generations and who personally knew Sterling believe that she was keeping a close eye on the renovations to make sure they were correct and appropriate. After the adobe once again opened to the public, a custodian at the museum inadvertently bumped into a table, almost knocking over some period pieces that were sitting on it, and heard the sound of high heels running toward her and then retreating when nothing actually fell from the table.

Also from cryptic79 comes another tale, of a custodian who said that she was cleaning the windows outside in the courtyard and having trouble getting the streaks out when she "felt something really cold on my back and something like ice and stuff on my neck." As she turned around, she saw a shadowy figure floating across the garden. It threw her a chilling glare as it evaporated into the opposite wall. "It was about 3:30 in the afternoon. The whole house was closed; nobody in the restrooms; nobody in the rooms, only myself….I looked around. I'm sure it was a ghost…. Maybe Mrs. Sterling?"

According to one more story from cryptic79's blog post, one afternoon, an Avila museum volunteer approached a woman who seemed to be concentrating on something in the garden. The volunteer asked the woman if everything was OK, and the woman responded, "Yes, but there is somebody who is not comfortable at all." The guest then pointed to another woman standing in the garden and said, "There's that lady, right in the middle of

Quite a few restoration workers and guests have seen spirits in the dining room, and many believe that Christine Sterling herself keeps an eye on the adobe.

the garden, walking back and forth like she's nervous....She feels something is wrong." Could the lady in the garden have been picking up on the spirit of Francisco Avila or Christine Sterling? Perhaps both?

Since Olvera Street opened as a tourist location, realizing the fantasized image Christine Sterling created, it has been mired in controversy. That controversy continues to this day and was brought into relief in 1990 when the City of Los Angeles and the Getty Museum restored a mural by Mexican Communist Party member and artist David Alfaro Siqueiros. The mural, first unveiled in 1932, *Tropical America: Oppressed and Destroyed by Imperialism*, was so radical that the Mexican population was shocked by its message, and Sterling was so outraged that the mural was ordered whitewashed four years after its unveiling. Siqueiros was eventually exiled from the United States after his direct involvement in an assassination attempt on Leon Trotsky.

Some historians have argued that the Los Angeles Plaza Historic District is nothing more than a fantasy Spanish marketplace that should not be celebrated, but they also admit that the area remains the birthplace of the city and for that it holds a place of significance, regardless of the fact that it is purely a romanticized, manufactured streetscape. Others, like Angeliz, have a more accepting philosophy regarding Olvera Street, "It is [a place of pride] probably going back to the Californians' days. We're talking about 1818, so." Another tour guide put it this way: "I mean, this *is* where they founded Los Angeles." Angeliz went on to say that the history here is not only the obvious Mexican history but an Indigenous history as well. After 206 years have passed and millions of folks have come to Olvera Street and the Avila Adobe, we owe it to Francisco and his two Marias as well as Christine Sterling to value the history above the fantasy, remember the people and keep their dream alive.

CHAPTER 4

PICO HOUSE PLUS TWO

The Pico House at Olvera Street is one of those buildings that cannot be written about as a single unit. This is because the historic Merced Theater and the Masonic Lodge are attached to the old hotel, and each has its own unique history. The Masonic Lodge itself is, according to Olvera Street lore, the oldest commercial building in Los Angeles, the Merced Theater was the first theater in the city and the Pico House was the most luxurious hotel in Los Angeles at a time when the city was emerging from its infancy. All three of these places were connected, with the hotel and theater having a direct corridor between them so hotel guests could simply walk through the passageway into the lobby of the Merced. The Masonic Lodge was connected later, with a common wall and egress into the upper lodge from a stairway in the back of the lodge and hotel. The ground floor was used for commerce, while the second floor housed Masonic Lodge No. 42. These three locations are connected by more than walls, roofs and stairways; they are also said to be connected by the spirits that seem to haunt these buildings: many of these may be the same specters, moving between the corridors of the structures as well as the ether that surrounds them.

What we now call the Masonic Hall building at 416 Main Street was originally built in 1858, by owners who ran a carpentry and furniture business on the ground floor. It is said that one of their specialties happened to be making very fine caskets for the wealthy of the city and decent coffins for the less well-to-do. To help pay the bills and keep the business going, they rented out the upper floor to the Masons for twenty dollars per month. The Masons

Pico Hotel. *Historic American Buildings Survey and Cris Stoffenback, via Library of Congress.*

loved the brick structure and the balcony, which had ornate ironwork railings, and they felt lucky to have such a large place to house Masonic Lodge No. 42. *Los Angeles Times* reporter Timothy Turner wrote in 1936, "That so small a building was a hall, then considered a spacious meeting place, is proof of the small scale of everything in those days." Several notable citizens of the time were Masons of this hall, including Alpheus Hall, the city's first elected mayor, and Benjamin Wilson, grandfather of World War II hero General George S. Patton.

In the early days of the hall's existence, something happened that is rare among the lodges: two Masons, one with the rank of Worshipful Master, became embroiled in what have been called "non-fraternal feelings" for another Mason. Two Masons having a conflict was not unusual; however, this conflict rose to the level of a duel between the two, which, to say the least, is frowned upon within the Masonic Order. According to historian Hilliard Dorsey, Worshipful Master Harris Newmark, a "typical Western character with a fiery temper," challenged another Mason to a duel. Each of the combatants "suffered a severe wound," and "both the Worshipful Master and his enemy were expelled from the order." Even though this occurred in 1854, four years before the Masons moved into their new hall, this event became a defining moment in the lodge's history.

As renters, the Masons had little control over things within the building itself, and several complaints arose about things they found all but unbearable, the worst being what was called the "travelling chandelier." It seems that interior lighting was a problem within the early El Pueblo, and because of this, churches, businesses and even individuals would borrow the chandelier that hung in the Masonic lodge. There were times that the lodge would have to meet by candlelight when they discovered the chandelier was once again missing. If that wasn't bad enough, the upper floor of the building had only five windows and four doors, which were woefully inadequate during the hot summer months and didn't provide nearly enough ventilation or cooling. Mix in the privacy sought by all Masonic lodges, and this all became intolerable. By 1868, the Masons had had enough and moved into a new location a few blocks away. They would eventually move into a new lodge that was built for them in Santa Monica, where Masonic Lodge No. 42 remains to this day. The building on Main Street, now known as Masonic Hall, began a new chapter—but not one that was destined to keep the building going into the future.

In the 1880s, the building became known for its real estate firms, and a self-proclaimed "capitalist" by the name of H.L. Flash. However, as time passed, these businesses moved south into the new business district around

The Pico House (*left*), Merced Theater (*center*) and Masonic Lodge (*right*). All three are said to be very haunted, possibly by some of the same spirits.

Temple Street. As the El Pueblo Plaza began to decline, the Masonic Hall saw an influx of bars and pawnshops, with the second floor becoming a roominghouse and, unofficially, a brothel. *Los Angeles Times* writer Turner, who visited in 1936, described the building during its time as a "boardinghouse" in the 1920s: "The proprietress kept canaries and an impudent parrot which she put on the balcony in appropriate weather as she sat in the doorway and combed her hair or peeled potatoes, as the occasion required." Turner visited again in 1936. "As one passes this old building," he wrote, "two smells assail the nose. One is emitted from the barbershop, which occupies half the street level, a smell of perfumes and lotions....The smell from the opposite half is of chili pepper, coffee and frijoles being fried with cheese, for it is a mart of victuals." The building was also used, according to Turner, by a sign painter, "who puts roses, if urged, on his signs and who has the soul, if not the technique of a Grand Master."

However, as the 1940s came and went, the Masonic Hall was slated for destruction to make way for the 101 Freeway. It was here that the Masons—even though they had only occupied the building for ten years and had left because of conditions they detested—stepped in to save their old lodge and the building that now bore their name. Lobbying the city and state, they successfully made their case and saved the structure and associated buildings from being sideswiped by the 101. In a victory for the new historic preservation movement, it was acquired by the El Pueblo. The Masonic Hall at Olvera Street, and its ghosts, had been saved.

It is said that the Masonic Hall is haunted by the same spirits that haunt the Pico House Hotel and the Merced Theater. While it is possible, no one is really sure if that is the case; all we do know is that it is haunted. This author has had the privilege of investigating this location, and although not much activity took place the night of the investigation, there were certainly some strange occurrences during my time in the old Masonic meeting room. I had the pleasure of investigating with paranormal legend Richard Senate, who had brought his dowsing rods with him in an attempt to get the spirits to manipulate them in communication. While our group asked random questions of the spirits, the rods did move in what appeared to be direct answers to our queries. At one point, one of the investigators asked if there were any Masons present in the hall, and the rods began to actually spin. It was obvious that even Richard Senate was surprised by this, by the look on his face. Besides the dowsing rods seemingly acting as they were meant to react, the only other strange things that happened could have simply been the sounds of an old building in the winter air.

With only these small windows, the Masonic Hall was sweltering in the summer months.

Reports from this building run the gamut, from strange voices calling out to those in the hall and those walking past on the sidewalk to strange lights that appear out of nowhere and move around the inside of the building until they simply fade away. Many believe that this might be a few of the spirits of the Chinese men some think were killed nearby and have since moved into the Masonic Hall. We may never know who the spirits are, but it is hoped that one day we will have an answer, perhaps from the ghosts themselves.

In the years since the late 1940s, the Masonic Hall has fallen into disrepair. The Masons did rededicate the building as a Masonic museum and had filled it with memorabilia and other museum pieces, but since it was declared seismically unfit many years ago, the building has been unoccupied and vacant. The outside of the building was beautifully restored, but the seismic retrofit and interior remain incomplete and the building unusable. Although the exterior has been featured in quite a few TV shows and movies, the ongoing recession along with the depressed economy has made further upgrades hard to come by. As the Masonic Hall is the oldest commercial building in Los Angeles, let us all hope that one day, this historic piece of LA comes back to us in all its splendor.

The Merced Theater

Although often called the first theater in Los Angeles, the Merced Theater was in fact the first theater built for only that purpose. The Temple Theater, just down the street, was actually the first, but because it was built mostly for retail rather than theater activity, the Merced has assumed the title—mostly. Sandwiched between the Masonic Hall to the south and the Pico House (built the same year as the Merced Theater) on the north, the theater was even more elaborate than the Pico House and would become one of Los Angeles' most notable early buildings. Maybe because of its proximity to the other buildings or simply because of the somewhat turbulent history of the theater itself, the building is notable not only for its design but for its spirit activity as well.

Opened the same year as the Pico House Hotel, the Merced Theater was created by Swiss immigrant and merchant William Abbott. Abbott had moved to Los Angeles from Indiana in 1849 and set up his furniture-making business after purchasing property near the Pueblo de la Reina de Los Angeles. Abbott began attending and giving parties as a way to meet all the local businessmen and soon established himself as a member of the city's elite. In 1858, Abbott fell in love with and married Maria Merced Garcia, who would become the inspiration for the theater and its name. Having always been interested in theater, Abbott wanted to bring the arts to Los

The Merced Theater. *Historic American Buildings Survey, via Library of Congress.*

Angeles and had been saving money to create his own place where its citizens could come and enjoy shows, plays and other forms of live entertainment. It took him a while to gather the funds, but by 1869, Abbott was ready to build his dream.

Abbott hired the same architect who had designed the Pico House, already under construction next door. The Merced Theater building would have three distinct uses. The ground floor would house Abbott's furniture and woodworking business, the second floor would become the four-hundred-seat theater and living space would be built on the third floor for himself and his family. The theater opened its doors in December 1870, as reported in the *Los Angeles Star*: "The opening of the new [Abbott's] theater will take place on Friday, December 30, 1870, when a grand vocal and instrumental concert will be given by the 21st Regiment (Wilmington) Band, assisted by several well-known amateurs, who have kindly volunteered their services." It would be another month before the theater would host its first play, a performance of *Fanchon the Cricket*, a melodrama by Augustus Waldauer adapted from the novel *La Petite Fadetta* (1849).

The Merced was the center of theatrical interest in Los Angeles from its opening until 1876. Its decline can be directly traced to the opening of the Woods Opera House four doors south of the Merced Theater. Even though the Merced was the first, it was not designed strictly as a theater; the Woods Opera House was. Where the Merced housed a cabinet business and the owners' living space, the new opera house was built as a pure theater; because of this, theatergoers flocked to the new venue from the moment it opened. Then, as a smallpox outbreak occurred in Los Angeles, the Merced Theater finally closed its doors in 1877. After its closure as a theater, the Merced offered its services as an informal entertainment venue. Through the 1880s, the Merced's reputation began to wane, as folks came to think of it as a place where "disrespectful dances" took place. It is said that the theater became a haven for the gay community, and as homosexuality was not well received in the late 1800s and early 1900s, the theater's fortunes lessened even more.

The building continued to support retail establishments on the ground floor, but over the years, the second-floor theater would become a Salvation Army hall and, later, an athletic club, when those establishments left. The second floor and the third-floor residence were subdivided for use as a roominghouse. As the years passed and this area of LA began to move into poverty, the Merced Theater building declined as well. When one of the stores (Barker and Allen, forerunner of Barker Bros. furniture chain) left,

This ground-floor shop in the Merced Theater building once housed the owner's furniture and cabinet store.

different businesses began to fill the retail space, such as a barbershop, a liquor wholesaler and a liquor store. Today, none remain. For the last few decades, the Merced Theater has remained vacant other than the barber until he, too, could no longer sustain his business. However, in that same timeframe, in the 1960s, the building's façade was restored. Additional work was done in the 1980s for seismic retrofitting along with installing new sprinkler, alarm and electrical systems. The City of Los Angeles has been looking to turn the theater building into a public access TV station for LA CityView 35.

The Merced Theater has been empty and unused for decades. Only construction workers, city inspectors and fire and safety personnel have been inside this historic building—that is, the only living people. The ghosts of the Merced, however, are said to be not only still haunting the theater but also quite active. As the theater is connected to the Pico House, it is believed that many of the spirits that haunt the old hotel move between the Pico House and the Merced Theater. It is not altogether clear if this is fact; however, Pio Pico has supposedly been seen on the roof of the Merced as well as his own building. Many of the construction workers doing their job inside the theater have reported hearing what is believed to be an actual show being performed on the now-missing stage; however, on inspection,

The second and third floors of the Merced held the theater and living space, respectively.

the sound simply ceases. On occasion, once the worker has left the room, the sounds start up once more.

The Abbott family lived on the third floor of the Merced Theater and, by all accounts, were quite happy there. After the venue closed its doors and William Abbot passed away in 1879, the census showed that the rest of the family was still living in the theater in the mid- to late 1880s; by this, it seems obvious how they felt about the place. This may be why many folks claim to see the family still "living" there to this day. There have been reports of not only hearing the children, in their younger years, still playing in the upstairs living area but also of actually hearing quarrels between Merced and William Abbott. As strange as this may seem, it is somehow comforting to think that married couples, even in death, still have spats; this should confirm that these same couples still feel love and have their softer side after death as well. Many have gone to investigate these sounds, but as they near the upper floor, they find that all is once again quiet on the marriage front.

Shadow figures are plentiful within the confines of the Merced Theater building, as are the sounds of disembodied voices, footsteps and strange light anomalies. Ghost hunters who have ventured into the building and those who've simply snapped pictures through the ground floor windows have discovered strange images and orbs when they return home to look at their pictures. Even though orbs are now and always will be controversial, one has to wonder at the sheer number caught here. The Merced Theater is long gone, and only the building remains to impart its history to us. I am glad that this historic theater has been preserved for future generations to learn from and enjoy. Hopefully, someday, we may be able to investigate this wonderful structure and learn its history from those who actually lived it and seem to still be present to this day.

PICO HOUSE HOTEL

There are few Angelinos who do not know the name Pio Pico. Pico was a legendary figure in the early days of California and especially the Los Angeles and South Bay areas. Known for his mixed heritage, Pico was of Italian, Spanish, African and Native American descent; his parents came to Alta California from Sinaloa, Mexico. The Pico, Dominguez, Sepulveda and Cabrillo families have been immortalized throughout the state by streets, municipal buildings, parks and whole cities that bear their names.

The Pico House Hotel was the most luxurious hotel in LA at the time it was built.

In Los Angeles, perhaps the most celebrated name is that of Pio Pico. Even Pico's old, haunted hotel in the Olvera Street Plaza is still well known—for its ghosts.

Born in the San Gabriel Mission in 1801, Pio was his parents' fourth child and grew up with two brothers and seven sisters. He spent most of his youth in San Diego, while his military father was assigned to the Presidio there. When his father died in 1819, he left Pio, his mother and siblings with no money or land, so nineteen-year-old Pio opened his own small store in San Diego selling shoes, furniture, goods and liquor. By 1823, he had made enough money to build his family a ten-room adobe; he and his family moved into their new home in 1824. Pico continued to build his wealth and, more importantly, his business connections. This would lead Pico to become governor of Alta California in 1832 and again in 1845 (Pio Pico was the last Mexican governor of Alta California before the United States gained control of the territory). During the Mexican American War, Pico attempted to raise troops, money and supplies to help fight off the Americans, but in 1846, he was forced to flee to Mexico to avoid capture by the advancing U.S. troops; he also went to ask the Mexican government for more military support.

After the war, Pico was one of only a very few who were able to hold onto their land, and he used his political influence to build a vast land empire. In

"Old Mission of San Gabriel," circa 1885. *From the New York Public Library.*

1850, Pico purchased 8,891 acres from the heirs of Don Juan Crispin Perez and named his new rancho El Ranchito (the little rancho). To help win over the new American politicos, Pico and the other dons would often entertain in grand style, holding festivals, weddings and other galas and inviting not only family and friends but also those in power whom they believed could help them along the way. During this time, Pico added a mill, a corral, a chapel and wells, along with gardens, fruit trees, grape vines and a canal to provide water to the home.

Pico was well known for his generosity, and those folks who stayed for a few weeks found that all their needs were taken care of while visiting the Pico rancho, right down to trays of coins left around the adobe so his guests didn't have to spend their own money if heading into town. By 1855, Pio and his brother Andres had expanded the rancho to 532,000 acres and become two of the richest men in California. Pico made most of his money with cattle, selling beef and hides, but also by selling tallow to passing gold prospectors heading north. When a destructive drought hit California in the early to mid-1860s and killed off many of Southern California's herds, Pico began selling oats, barley, grapes and other fruits to help counter the loss of cattle

You can see the Pico House in this photo of the original Plaza Firehouse. *Historic American Buildings Survey, via Library of Congress.*

sales. By the late 1860s, Pico, looking to expand his fortunes and seeing an opportunity in the growing downtown section of nearby Los Angeles, came up with the idea of building a grand hotel that would bear his name.

Pico wanted not only a grand hotel but also one that would be known around the country and, perhaps, the world. He envisioned the most luxurious hotel in all Southern California, and what he built may have been the finest hotel of its time in the entire state. Pico knew that what he proposed would not come cheap, and the final cost of the Pico House Hotel would ring in at a whopping $80,000 (roughly $2.1 million today). What Pico got for his money was a magnificent Italianate Victorian masterpiece designed by California's very first professional architect, Ezra F. Kysor. Pico and his brother had to sell most of their landholdings to pay for the Pico House, which shows how much faith they had in the endeavor: it was a case of success or poverty. The hotel opened to a lot of fanfare, and when folks first saw the hotel, they stood in awe. The Pico House boasted eighty bedrooms, all with running water and gas lighting. It also had twenty-one parlors for entertaining and socializing, all arranged around a central courtyard replete with a fountain and a bird aviary; the courtyard also featured an elegant French café, all behind an exterior finished to look like blue granite. There was even a shuttle for guests that took them to and from the hotel to the nearby train stations. Pico had indeed accomplished his goal of creating the finest hotel in Southern California and the Southwest.

Having already sold most of his holdings (he still owned his beloved El Ranchito), Pico was dependent on the Pico House for the majority of his income. Always one to keep things fresh and new in his grand hotel, Pico spent too much money buying things he fancied not only for the hotel but also for himself. As we have seen in his treatment of guests at his rancho, his generosity was without equal; however, this generosity, mixed with gambling and a penchant for horse racing, became a problem, and overspending on things not needed caused his riches to fade rapidly. By 1880, only ten years after the hotel opened, Pico was in foreclosure and was forced to sell all his properties—except his beloved rancho. The Pico House was sold to the San Francisco Savings and Loan Company for only $16,000. Pico would go on to live at his rancho, doing very little of the entertaining he was known for, until 1892, the year his land was stolen from him. Pico, never having learned to read or speak English, was vulnerable to Bernard Cohn, an unscrupulous American lawyer, who cheated Pico out of his land and kicked him out of his own property and ranch house. Pico was forced to load up what few possessions he had left and move in with his adopted daughter, Joaquina Moreno. Pico lived with his daughter for two years before he passed away, penniless, on September 11, 1894.

As for the Pico House Hotel, it changed hands numerous times over the years. In 1882, the hotel found itself so overbooked it had to outsource rooms across the street to accommodate its guests, many of whom complained about not being given the rooms they paid for in the hotel they booked. This, combined with much of the city's business activity moving south, caused a decline in the hotel's guest list. By the start of the 1900s, the hotel was all but empty. Over the years, the Pico House housed a variety of commercial businesses, apartments, events and even a pool hall, and in all that time, the once-glamorous building fell into a state of decay. In 1953, the State of California stepped in by taking over the building, however they didn't begin renovations until 1981 and then again in 1992. There is still much to be done, but once the Pico House was added to the National Historic Landmark and California Historical Landmark lists, its future became much brighter. Now, as part of the El Pueblo de Los Angeles Historical Monument, the building

The Old Plaza Firehouse today.

is seeing guests again—although rarely—through events, historical tours and even ghost walks and ghost tours of the building. I am sure the ghosts that reside there are happy to have new guests come to visit them—at least we hope they are happy about it.

Many consider the Pico House to be the most haunted place in Los Angeles. I will not enter into the argument, as Olvera Street alone, near where the Pico House resides, also has many wonderfully haunted locations. Needless to say, there are few who dispute the fact that the Pico House is very haunted. It would seem that even those working at the El Pueblo de Los Angeles have had a few run-ins with the spirits of the Pico House, causing one to quit outright and another to put in for an immediate transfer. Others, of course, seem to not be overly bothered by the recurrence of paranormal activity, while a few seem to enjoy it.

There is a story, told to the *Ghost Adventures* crew during filming, that once, during a movie shoot, one of the security guards working at the Pueblo one night found so much spiritual activity that he was running all over the building trying to figure out what was happening, paranormal or mundane. It was said that during the night, the security guard began hearing strange noises on the second floor. When he went upstairs, he didn't hear a thing, but as he turned to leave, he saw a toolbox begin to shake violently. As he approached the toolbox, it started shaking even more and then began to spin wildly, like it was on a spindle. He then began to hear more noises off to his left, but instead of going over to investigate, he descended the stairs back down to the ground floor. When he reached the ground floor, all the noise stopped above him, and he figured that the ordeal was over.

A little later that evening, the security guard began hearing noises on the third floor and went up to investigate the area. He passed the second-floor landing quickly as he didn't want a repeat of his earlier experience. When he arrived at the third-floor landing, he stood there for a few moments, but the sound he had been hearing had stopped. He walked around the third floor to make sure there was no one hiding anywhere, and once he was sure there was no intruder, he started down the stairs, heading back to his post on the ground floor. He was only halfway down the stairway when he felt someone kick him in his back so hard that he almost fell the rest of the way down the staircase. He was still high enough that if he had fallen, he could have been seriously injured. To his credit, the security guard finished the rest of his shift, somewhat apprehensively, but when his shift was over and daylight once again came to the Pueblo, the guard promptly quit, never to return to the Pico House.

Another incident told to the *Ghost Adventures* crew by the security guards working on Olvera Street had to do with the security cameras that are

One can see why Pico built his hotel where he did, adjacent to the plaza where LA citizens congregated.

pointed in the direction of the Pico House. One guard who was working the night shift in the camera monitoring room spotted a "man with a long white beard" walking along the roof of the Pico House Hotel. He watched the man for a few moments and then headed over to the old building and made his way to the roof. Once he got there, there was no sign of anyone having been up on the roof: no footprints, nothing amiss or disturbed. It was as if the man had just vanished. The following day, the guard was back at work when a coworker brought in a flyer for a history event that was going to take place at the Pico House. As the event celebrated the history of Pio Pico, his picture was featured prominently on the flyer. When the guard who had watched the man walking on the roof saw the picture of Pico, the look that came over him caused his coworker to ask what was wrong. The guard looked at his friend and told him that the man on the flyer was the same man he had seen the night before, walking on the roof. The guard promptly put in for a transfer.

Another employee told the *Ghost Adventures* crew that one morning as she was opening the museum, she headed over to a nearby light switch, but before she could get there, she noticed a shadow right next to her. She stopped dead in her tracks, and the shadow stopped with her. The shadow figure was so close to her that she simply froze in place. She didn't know if it was the shadow that was keeping her from moving or if it was her own fear, but after a few moments, she realized that she needed to get moving. She didn't know what would happen if she just stood there, but she wasn't about to stay and find out. She said that she figured the lights would dispel the shadow figure, so she all but ran to turn them on. Once the switch was flipped, the shadow was gone, and all seemed normal inside the Pico House.

I myself have had the pleasure of investigating the Pico House with my friend Joe Ruffulo right after the *Ghost Adventures* team had been there, so soon afterward that the crew's camera marks were still taped to the floor of the hotel. Not much occurred during our investigation of the hotel other than a few simple class B and C EVPs; we actually caught more evidence during our investigation at the Masonic lodge that same night. It was the same for our friends, the Paranormal Housewives, during their investigation later on; they, however, did get a bit of evidence in both the hotel and the basement area. The team had split into two groups, with one heading upstairs and the other down into the basement. The group that had gone up stopped on the second floor and decided to investigate there first. While conducting their investigation, the women distinctly heard footsteps on the floor above them. As the other group was in the basement, they knew there was nobody on the third floor. As the women went up to investigate the sounds above them, an "overpowering and nasty smell came from nowhere" as soon as they set foot on the third floor. As Paranormal Housewife Kristen Thorne stated in a rather amusing fashion, "Horrible smells make me nervous, as some consider them to be signs of a demonic presence…but I won't go that far; and NO, it was not the result of indigestion or unladylike emissions."

Almost at the same moment, the other investigators in the basement were experiencing their own unusual happenings. While here, Paranormal Housewife Kimberly picked up a strange audio EVP. "I usually don't say what it is I hear, but in this case, I will say that I hear more than the other ladies." She went on to say that in the recording, you can hear another voice under that of Marsha (another Paranormal Housewife), a voice whispering something unintelligible, as well as a clear response to a question that Marsha had asked only moments earlier. Kimberly also said that she could hear talking between those two points on the recorder, although what was being said could not be understood. Paranormal Housewife Erin said, "As investigators, we look to get two or three things happening at once or close to each other; we feel that is more concrete evidence." They certainly seemed to meet this goal while investigating the Pico House.

Other paranormal phenomenon that occurs on a regular basis at the Pico House is that the hotel room doors along the courtyard walkways on every floor have a tendency to open and slam shut with no one nearby, and as they all automatically latch when they close, it is an odd thing to watch them move on their own. Visitors and security alike report the sound of footsteps at all hours of the day, but it seems to be more common during the late-night hours. There are many reports of figures leaning over the inner courtyard balconies as if enjoying their stay without a care in the world. Shadows moving along the walkways and in rooms are common, and it is said that every once in a while, the sounds of a party can be heard coming from inside the empty building. With all the activity reported at the Pico House, maybe it does deserve the title of most haunted in Los Angeles, and maybe, just maybe, Pio Pico himself is still holding his galas, still hosting his guests and still caring less about money than being generous to his friends in death as he was in life.

CHAPTER 5

LOS ANGELES UNION STATION

The sound of the wheels rolling across the rails, the lonesome whistle of the train as it rides on through the night and the steam issuing from the railcars as the locomotive pulls into the station: all of these bring to mind the romance and adventure that train travel once elicited in the minds of the American public. Today, nothing keeps these images more in focus than Los Angeles' Union Station. During the golden age of train travel, railway stations were built in most major cities. Some of them were mundane buildings that were simply functional, while others were grand structures designed to impress travelers and make them feel as if they were about to step onboard one of Europe's legendary trains. Most of these opulent depots are gone, with only one or two still standing, but thanks to Los Angeles, what has been called the most beautiful station ever built is not only still standing but also still serving intracontinental rail lines along with thousands of commuters on a daily basis, not to mention a spectral passenger or two as well.

Los Angeles Union Station has been called the most beautiful and picturesque train station ever built. Today, it also holds the moniker "Last of the Great Train Stations." Both descriptors seem even more amazing when one realizes that Los Angeles Union Station was one of the last great stations—if not *the* last—to be built. Like a lot of things built in LA in the early days, Union Station began with controversy and racial discord.

As we have seen, the Chinese massacre by an angry mob in 1871 both set in motion steps to quell any further violence and created more

LA's Union Station is not only considered one of the most beautiful train stations in the United States—it's also dubbed the "last of the great train stations."

animosity toward the Chinese population of LA. In one attempt to stem the violence, the city renamed the street where Chinatown stood—from Calle de los Negros to Los Angeles Street—in 1877. Through the whole ordeal, the Chinese populace never wavered from their commitment to not only Chinatown but also the area as a whole. However, there were factions within the community and the city government that were anti-Chinese and would continually work to remove the Chinese from the city. By the early 1900s, the city was growing—and with it a call to consolidate the three rail depots the city had in proximity to one another into one grand union station. The anti-Chinese forces were pushing for the new depot to be placed within the boundaries of Chinatown, thereby displacing that community.

The first major railroad to come to Los Angeles was the Southern Pacific in 1876, when it connected LA with San Francisco via Tehachapi. The second was the Atchison, Topeka & Santa Fe in May 1887 and finally, in 1905, the Union Pacific, when it completed the rail lines of the Los Angeles & Salt Lake Railroad. With three countrywide rail companies competing for passengers in a city that was seeing a population boom, congestion in the downtown area was beginning to be a problem, and with all three serving different passenger terminals, that congestion was only compounded. The idea of a union passenger terminal came about shortly after the turn of the century but began to gather steam around 1910, and in 1911, the LA City Council authorized a study for the project. The three railroads were wholeheartedly against the idea and immediately began fighting the proposal. The railroads began pushing their idea of elevated rail lines that would reduce congestion while making it easier for their passengers to arrive at their respective depots—but many folks, especially East Coast transplants, fought the idea of "four miles of hideous, clattering, dusty, dirty, dangerous, street-darkening overhead trestles," as the *Los Angeles Times* described them. By 1916, the city council had filed suit demanding a single terminal, which set off a prolonged, ten-year battle with the railroads that eventually ended up in the U.S. Supreme Court, where the justices ruled in favor of the city. With the loss of their court case, combined with a vote taken by the people of Los Angeles in 1926, the railroads had no choice but to build a single terminal.

As Stan L. Bottles wrote in his 1991 book *Los Angeles and the Automobile: The Making of a Modern City*,

> *What began in 1916 as an attempt to improve the city's railroad stations had evolved by 1926 into a major controversy over the nature of the city's public-transit system. When the electorate finally voted down the railroads' proposal, the city was left with the same problems it had before. Downtown traffic was increasing, and interurbans stall in congestion, and the city lacked a plan for improving its public-transit facilities.*

In 1926, a measure was put on the ballot for a vote, and voters were given a choice between the elevated railways or the construction of a union station where all rail lines would operate. The results were overwhelming, with 61.3 percent voting for the union station. In a second vote on the same ballot, the people chose the Los Angeles Plaza as the site for the new terminal. This vote, however, was much narrower, as only 51.1 percent of the electorate voted for this site.

Now that it had been decided to build a union terminal, the wrangling began over exactly where the new station would be built. Those who had been actively working for the removal of the Chinese began lobbying and eventually won their battle to have the new station located in what was, at this time, Chinatown.

Beginning in the early 1930s, the Chinese population was moved to what would eventually become New Chinatown (which opened in 1938).

The ticketing area shows off the Art Deco beauty of the LA depot.

Like always, the Chinese took it all in stride and, instead of complaining, began to build their new area into what would become a premier Chinese cultural center in the United States. It would be thirteen years before the new terminal was completed, but it finally opened in May 1939, to much fanfare and a few minor protests. A three-day celebration attended by half a million residents became one of the largest events to date in Los Angeles.

Union Station was designed by the father-and-son architect team of John and Donald Parkinson; the duo blended three different styles into a masterpiece of Mission Revival, Spanish Colonial and Art Deco that would eventually be called the most beautiful train station in the country. The final cost of the complex would come out at just above $11 million, which was almost exactly what the estimates for construction had been many years earlier. Unfortunately, John Parkinson would not live to see the completion of his and his son's marvelous design, as he passed away in December 1935. Many call Los Angeles Union Station the duo's seminal work. First called the Los Angeles Union Passenger Terminal, the station served not only the three major railroads but the Pacific Electric "Red Cars" and the Los Angeles Railway's streetcars as well. This allowed rail passengers to easily transfer to and from local public transit service. From the moment Union Station opened, it was a huge success.

Left: When the station opened, no amenity was overlooked, including a shoeshine stand.

Opposite: Amtrak took over the U.S. rail service in 1971 and still operates at LA Union Station today.

Unfortunately, as Union Station opened, other, faster forms of transportation were on the rise, and the station's success didn't last long. The war in Europe began just four months after the station opened, and the United States was dragged into the conflict with the Japanese bombing of Pearl Harbor on December 7, 1941. World War II actually aided the new terminal as thousands of U.S. troops were deployed around the country and the world, most traveling by train and many coming to Los Angeles for deployment to the Pacific Theater of Operations (PTO). After the war ended, with freeways being constructed (ironically enough, from a bond issue approved on the same ballot as the union station vote in 1926) to cater to the burgeoning car culture and air travel on the rise, the number of rail passengers coming through Union Station began to decline at an alarming rate. What had once been a crowded twenty-four-hours-a-day, seven-days-a-week rail terminal that thousands of folks traveled through on a daily basis became a forgotten, all but abandoned depot in the heart of a thriving city.

868

By 1970, the three big passenger railroads that the station had been built to service had cut their routes to the point that it was rare to see a train arriving in LA, and by 1971, they no longer serviced passengers at all, replaced by the new nationally funded Amtrak. Amtrak did increase its train schedule to and from LA Union Station, but few folks were riding the rails in favor of the much faster, and cheaper, air travel. Things looked bleak for what was known as the Last of the Great Train Station, as plans were put forth to demolish the terminal in favor of housing and retail.

In 1971, when Amtrak took over the nation's passenger train routes, Union Station had become a shell of its former self. With few folks coming to ride the rails, the depot continued its steady decline, with the homeless finding shelter in its nooks and crannies. Its new owners decided that it might be best to tear down the old station. Even though Union Station had been designated Los Angeles Historic Cultural Monument 101 in 1972 and then added to the National Register of Historic Places and the California Register of Historic Resources in 1980, it was still uncertain what would ultimately happen with the complex. Then, in 1984, the Santa Fe Pacific Realty Corporation, which would oversee all non-railroad real estate interests for Santa Fe (the company was later renamed Catellus), developed two new business towers and an apartment complex on Union Station property, which actually helped save the train station from demolition.

Catellus recognized the growing interest in Amtrak and transit usage emanating from Union Station and figured the dual use of the property was just what the old terminal needed, and they were right. Union Station became a hub for folks arriving from all over the United States who came to Los Angeles for business and vacations and to see the sights in Hollywood, the beaches and the mountains of the area. Today, Los Angeles Union Station is once again seeing passengers coming in from all over the country, as well as thousands of commuters who ride the transit rails to and from their place of work. The terminal is also a hub for those flying out of town, as it serves as a commuter bus center for those heading to the various local and international airports in the area. Union Station is directly across the street from Olvera Street, the Pico House and the spot where the infamous Chinese riot began; this—combined with the fact that the massacre took place not in the plaza but on the grounds of Union Station—may be the reason that it could possibly be the most haunted train station in the country.

The site of the Chinese massacre has somehow, over the years, been transferred to El Pueblo de Los Angeles and the Pico House. Granted, the riot did begin near the plaza, but the horrendous acts of vigilante justice and

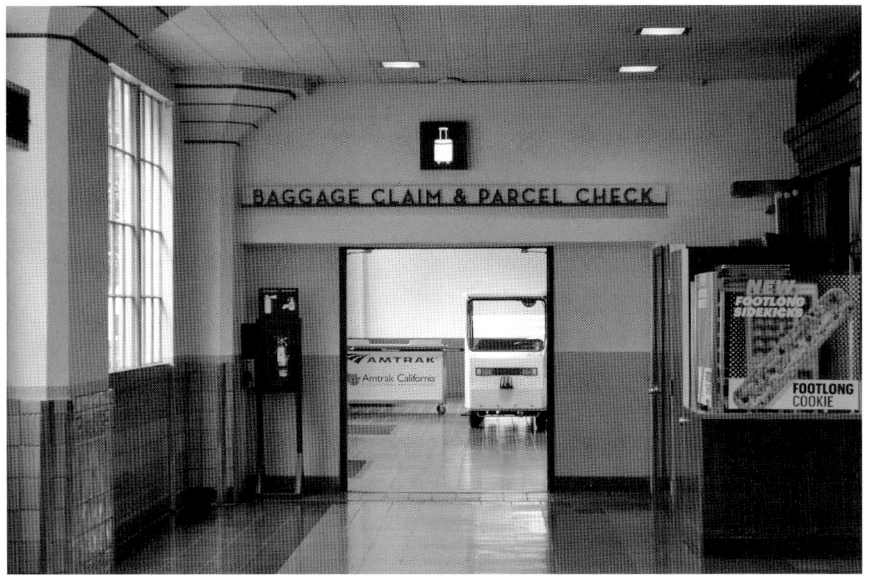

Although the "Trunk Murder" took place before Union Station opened, many believe they have seen the ghosts of those murdered in the baggage claim area.

the hangings of what were mostly innocent men took place on the grounds of what would become Union Station. This kind of act can and will leave a mark on the land that may never be cleaned or removed. Such an act alone can cause folks, especially those with a weak mind, to perform their own acts of barbarism and evil against those around them in the future, and Union Station has certainly seen its fair share of this during its lifespan. On occasion, things that happened before a place is even built can become a magnet for spirits who just need closure.

Take the case of Winnie Ruth Judd, the infamous "Trunk Murderess." She has sometimes been referred to as the "Tiger Woman" or the "Velvet Tigress." Winnie, whose father had been a Methodist minister, married Dr. William C. Judd, and they moved to Phoenix, where he set up his practice. William traveled quite a lot, which left Winnie alone most of the time, so she took a job as a medical secretary to help support herself and keep busy. She soon developed a friendship with Anne LeRoi, Hedvig "Sammy" Samuelson and a man by the name of Jack Halloran. The four became quite close, but Halloran and Judd became even closer and began having an affair. Halloran, even though he was sleeping with Judd, would still flirt with LeRoi and Samuelson, even when Judd protested. On October 16, 1931, Judd went over to her friend's duplex to confront her two female companions.

An argument ensued, and Judd shot and killed her two friends. To this day, it is still unclear whether LeRoi and Samuelson had firearms of their own, as Judd was also shot in the hand. After the killings, Judd gathered some surgical tools her husband kept at home and proceeded to cut up the bodies of LeRoi and Samuelson and stuff them into steamer trunks. Then she took a train from Phoenix to Los Angeles' Central Station (Southern Pacific's depot at the time). On arriving at Central Station, Judd left the trunks sitting outside, where three days later, a railroad worker, following a foul smell, discovered the trunks, blood dripping out from every seam. After a weeklong manhunt, Judd surrendered to police at a Los Angeles funeral home. She spent the rest of her life in and out of prison and mental wards.

Even though Union Station had yet to be built at the time of the murders, many folks have told tales of seeing the two dead women in and around the train depot. The story that the trunks were found at Union Station—eight years before the terminal had been built—is most likely due to confusion, as many news articles labeled Central Station as Union Station. As for the spirits of the two women, it may be a case of the two friends simply trying to get back home.

Another case with a link to Union Station has been called the most famous railroad murder in U.S. history—or, as most know it, the Lower Thirteen Murder. This case has so many twists and turns that we may never know who truly committed the crime or whether an innocent man went to the gas chamber. All we really know is that a beautiful young woman and a young Black man were taken from the earth, both by another's hand, and both may still be seen in Union Station. The tale began on January 23, 1943, as the West Coast Limited headed to Los Angeles from Seattle. At approximately four thirty in the morning, Martha Virginia James let out a bloodcurdling scream and called out, "Oh, my God, he's killing me!" from the lower sleeping berth in room 13. Moments later, the U.S. marine who had been sleeping in the berth right above her "chased a man he had seen near the dead woman's berth" to the end of the train but lost him there. The marine said that he had passed through the dining car while giving chase and asked the cook, who was "out of breath and sweating profusely" even though it "seemed cold in the kitchen," if he had seen anyone run through, to which the cook responded, "No." The cook would eventually be arrested, tried, convicted and executed for the crime. It is here things get murky.

The murder took place as the train rolled through Oregon near the town of Tangent. Officers used the description the marine gave them to hunt down the culprit, whom they believed was still on the train, and finally settled on

Right: This tunnel leads not only to the different tracks but also a commuter shopping area.

Below: Track 13 once had an abandoned, haunted train car sitting on its siding.

Robert E. Lee Folkes—the train's second cook and the man the marine said he spoke with in the kitchen—as their prime suspect. After Folkes's arrest in Los Angeles, where he lived, it is said that he was calm, cool and unfazed during questioning by LAPD officers. They set up a trap for him by claiming to have sent a picture of him to a woman who was molested on the same train twelve days before the murder (the rape actually had occurred) and telling Folkes she had positively identified him as her assailant. Records show that Folkes immediately broke down and admitted to killing James after the ruse. There is some speculation, however, that Folkes may have just been an easy mark for law enforcement, who were looking to pin the crime on an innocent Black man.

Many believe that not only would it have been all but impossible for a woman to be raped and murdered in a berth with a marine sleeping above her without waking him up but the culprit would also have been very stupid to attempt it. It also seems a bit odd that after James let out a scream, this same marine, having woken up and seen the murderer, was unable to, if not catch him outright, certainly keep up with him in a foot chase through the train. As for Folkes being covered in sweat and out of breath, we only have the marine's word for this. Many believe that the marine may have been the actual killer and framed Folkes to get away with the rape and murder. It is also very possible, considering the era, that police not only believed a White Marine, especially while World War II was still raging, over a Black man but also "interrogated" the Black man to the point of confession. We will most likely never know the truth about this case, but it would seem that neither James nor Folkes have been at rest since the incident took place.

There have been reports of seeing a spectral woman exiting the Amtrak Coast Starlight train when it pulls into Union Station. As this would be the same route that the West Coast Limited traveled, many believe that this spirit is that of Martha James. The ghost is only glimpsed for a split second directly on arrival of the Coast Starlight and is so quick that no detail can be discerned about it other than that it is a woman. Could this actually be James's spirit finally arriving at her destination? Folkes, on the other hand, has been seen wandering about Union Station as if lost or confused. He is seen wearing his cook's uniform or, on occasion, his pinstriped zoot suit he was fond of. Some have tried to approach him; however, like many spirits, he seems to notice the living and will simply vanish when approached. It is hoped that both spirits will someday find the peace in the afterlife that they deserve.

The old Harvey House restaurant (a fixture at many train stations that serviced the Santa Fe trains) is long gone from Union Station; however, the new eatery that has taken its place in modern times, Traxx, now serves fine food and fantastic cocktails. Originally designed by architect Mary Jane Coulter, who worked for the Harvey House company designing its concessions areas, once said that she wanted to create places where spirits would feel comfortable. Being fascinated by Native American culture and architecture, she may have been speaking about Native spirits, but it would seem that ghosts are also comfortable in the places she designed. Many Harvey Houses around the country are said to be extremely haunted, La Posada in Arizona and our own Harvey House here in Barstow, California, being two of the most "spirited," but it also seems that Union Station's eatery and bar, Traxx, also falls into the "haunted" category. Traxx is very close-lipped about the haunts, as is the entire Union Station management, but folks have talked about seeing spirits there working, dining and enjoying the wonderful food Traxx offers. Many Harvey Girls remain at the Harvey establishments that are still standing, and it would not be hard to believe that the girls' devotion to the business and the man who treated them as equals are still plying their trade at Union Station's modern eatery.

The old Harvey House Restaurant is said to be haunted, as is the new Traxx bar and grill inside the depot.

The beauty of LA Union Station is unmatched by any other train station in the United States.

From a man in a World War II military uniform who stands waiting for a companion who never arrives in the north courtyard and a strange moaning heard where the brutal lynching of innocent Chinese men took place just outside the entryway of the station itself—this train terminal may very well be the most haunted of its kind in the country. Haunted or not, this depot in the heart of downtown Los Angeles is certainly one of the most—if not *the* most—beautiful. From the terra-cotta tile that greets visitors on entering the building to the ornate Art Deco interior that has been said to "harken back to a time when rail travel was the way of style and grace and which imparts noir images right out of Sam Spade and *Casablanca*," Union Station is the perfect welcome to sunny Southern California. As Tom Zoellner writes in his book *Train*, "Certainly, I know of no other city in which arriving passengers leave the station through an open patio, filled with bright flowers, shady pepper trees and flanked with tall palms. The scheme undoubtedly originated with publicity men, but they have certainly hit upon the ideal introduction to Southern California." A perfect description for what truly is "the last of the great train stations."

CHAPTER 6

THE CURSE OF THE CECIL HOTEL

What does one say about a hotel built for business elites and well-to-do tourists that, almost from the time it opened, became a place of suicide and despair and was brought low only a couple of years into its existence before devolving into a place of mystery, death, murderers, the unhoused and the unwanted until finally becoming a place where, it is said, ghosts walk the hallways and rooms in a never-ending attempt to find their way home through the veil? All this and more has been the life of the Cecil Hotel in downtown Los Angeles. But over the years, those who stayed at the hotel never mentioned sleeping with ghosts or seeing them wandering the corridors or peering out the windows, watching the world go by—at least not until TV cameras came to visit. This author does not believe in curses per se, but if curses do exist, I would say that the Hotel Cecil, although possibly not haunted, may truly be cursed.

Designed by Loy Lester Smith for hotelier William Banks Hanner, the Hotel Cecil opened on December 20, 1924. The hotel was originally named the Metropolitan, but Hanner, in a nod to the famous Hotel Cecil in London, England, changed the name shortly before the Hotel Cecil opened. Built to cater to influential businessmen and well-to-do tourists, the hotel, close to rail, bus and public transit terminals, was well appointed for the time, featuring Beaux Arts styling mixed with a hint of Art Deco, and sported a marble lobby, stained glass and an opulent staircase that all came together in a way that exuded class and wealth. One thing the Hotel Cecil had working against it was the fact that not all the rooms had bathrooms or sinks. With

The Hotel Cecil, at the time it opened, was one of the grandest in LA.

seven hundred rooms on fourteen floors (of course, there was no thirteenth floor) to choose from, the cost of a room was dependent on its amenities. A room with only community bath facilities cost $1.50 a night, those with only a sink were $2.00, a room with a bath and sink cost $2.50 and one with a full bathroom would set you back $3.00. This setup was not convenient for many travelers and put the Hotel Cecil below many of its rivals in downtown LA.

William Hanner had invested $1 million in the construction of the hotel, which is the equivalent of $18 million today. Hanner may have thought the investment was worth it; however, neither he nor the rest of the world had any inkling that the stock market was about to crash and send the banking industry into default and the dreams of many a businessman into ruin. For five years after the Hotel Cecil opened, it played host to important business tycoons coming to the "Wall Street of the West," movers and shakers of industry and tourists both middle and upper class coming to Los Angeles to see the sights, catch a glimpse of the rising Hollywood film empire and take in the beautiful Southern California sunshine. All of that came to a sudden end on October 24, 1929, known as Black Thursday, the first of five days of the stock market crash. After the following Tuesday, known as Black Tuesday, the world was plunged into the Great Depression and the Hotel Cecil was all but finished.

With the collapse of the stock market, the "West Coast Wall Street" all but shut down, and although some businessmen still came to Los Angeles, they were now few and far between. Coupled with the complete loss of tourist dollars, the Hotel Cecil began to lose money in droves. As the Great Depression wore on, the area where the Hotel Cecil was located began to see an influx of the homeless, and soon, the entire area became the "Skid Row" section of downtown LA. When desperate people feel unwanted, many turn to crime, and as the poverty rises, so does alcohol addiction, violence and crime. Skid Row was no exception. To help keep the doors of the hotel open, the Cecil began to rent rooms at an extremely low rate for both short- and long-term stays. With its proximity to Skid Row, many of the homeless and those "selling their wares" would come to the Cecil, and the hotel soon garnered a reputation for sex peddlers, crime and illicit goods. One would think that the hotel's reputation, along with the Depression itself, would be reason enough for someone to take their own life, and as we will find out, the Hotel Cecil has a long list of suicides. However, the first recorded death at the Cecil was registered in 1927, a full two and a half years before the Great Depression hit.

Only three years after the hotel opened, Percy Ormond Cook checked into the Hotel Cecil after being kicked out of his house by his wife. It seems that the couple had been fighting, so Percy took up living in the Hotel Cecil while trying to patch things up with his wife. After it became clear he would never be able to reconcile with his wife and son, Percy put a gun to his head and pulled the trigger on January 22, 1927. Some look at this event as the beginning of a possible curse put on the hotel and property that is still in effect to this day. Many say that the despair Percy felt infected the building itself or that Percy's spirit, filled with an unending and unbearable depression, is somehow causing all the death and misery that has filled the Hotel Cecil since the day he took his own life. Whatever may have caused the unending destruction of human lives since then, no one can say there isn't something strange at work in the halls and walls of the hotel.

After the Cecil opened its doors to the denizens of Skid Row, it is understandable that these folks, many of whom had become homeless due to circumstances beyond their control, had become so overwhelmed that they would take their own lives. This, unfortunately, is part of human nature. However, even considering the criminal element now within the hotel, the sheer amount of death, murder, drug addiction and suicide that has gone on at the Cecil defies logic. In the 1930s alone, five guests died: four took their own lives and one death was ruled an accidental fall, although this could also have easily been a suicide. The first suicide of the 1930s took place in November 1931, as an article from the *Los Angeles Times* dated November 19, 1931, states, "Missing from his home in Manhattan Beach since last Saturday...W.K. Norton, age 46 was found dead in a hotel room at [the Cecil] yesterday morning. A number of capsules believed to have contained poison...had ended his life." There was no evidence or note about why he may have committed suicide. In September 1932, Benjamin Dodich was found by a maid with a self-inflicted gunshot wound to the head. No note or reason was given or ever found for why he took his life.

Another suicide, one that was a bit more gruesome, occurred in 1934, when Army Sergeant Louis D. Borden slit his own throat with a straight razor. As the *Los Angeles Times* reported on Friday, July 27, 1934, "His throat slashed, Louis D Borden, 53 years of age...died in a hotel room at [the Cecil] yesterday morning. Finding a razor by the body and farewell notes, reported Borden ended his own life because of ill health." The final suicide of the 1930s occurred when a marine by the name of Roy Thompson jumped from the hotel and landed on the skylight of another building. As the *Times* reported, "Leaving no note to explain his action, Roy Thompson, 35-year-old marine fireman, took what police termed a suicide leap from the fourteenth story of a downtown hotel [the Cecil]." The fourteenth floor of the Hotel Cecil would become the most notorious floor in the most notorious hotel in history.

Rounding out the deaths of the 1930s is that of Grace E. Margo. In 1937, Grace and boyfriend, M.W. Madison, a sailor onboard the USS *Virginia*, checked into the Hotel Cecil, and early the next morning, Grace was dead, having fallen from her window. The *Times* reported, "Police were unable to determine whether the woman had fallen or jumped from the hotel room. Telephone wires, ripped from poles in her descent, were entangled about her body." Her boyfriend was asleep at the time and couldn't give any information to the police or press. From the time the Hotel Cecil opened until the beginning of 1940, there were more strange occurrences and deaths there than any hotel should experience in its lifetime. In 1927, John Croneur was arrested in his room for running from police after stealing a diamond hairpin from the Rosslyn hotel. In 1929, thirty-three-year-old Dorothy Roberson was finally taken to a hospital after wandering around the hotel for three days, this after she tried to poison herself with medication prescribed after the death of her husband. Then there is the case of an elderly man being taken from the Cecil after drinking poisoned liquor that had already killed three other men. A truck driver was fatally pinned against the hotel wall by a large truck. All this occurred within the span of thirteen years.

The mayhem at the Hotel Cecil didn't end when the 1940s began; things may have actually gotten worse by some standards. One of the Cecil's long-term renters, an elderly man, tried to shoot himself in a local park. An elderly woman living at the hotel was found floating dead in the water at a nearby beach. A young bandit was arrested at the Cecil still carrying the note he had used in an armed robbery; the note read, "You are covered. Open the cash register and shell out. No tricks or else." One of the most horrendous and heartbreaking events to happen at the Hotel Cecil occurred in September 1944 when nineteen-year-old Dorothy Jean Purcell and her thirty-eight-year-old male companion, Ben Levine, checked into the Hotel Cecil. The couple had been at the hotel for several days when, in the early morning, Purcell began having abdominal pains. Not wanting to wake Levine, she left the room for the hotel bathroom, where she gave birth to a son. According to Purcell, she thought the baby boy was stillborn, so she threw the newborn child out of a window, went back to bed and never mentioned what had happened to her male companion. Purcell was eventually found not guilty of murder by reason of insanity and sent to a mental hospital.

The 1940s in Los Angeles was home to one of the grisliest unsolved murders of the twentieth century, that of the Black Dahlia. An urban legend has grown up connecting the Hotel Cecil with the Dahlia that is simply nothing more than a story made up by a man who hated his father. The urban legend says that Elizabeth Short (the Black Dahlia) exited the Biltmore Hotel where she had been dropped off and walked to her favorite bar at the Hotel Cecil. She then ran from the bar, seeking help from a female officer walking her beat, but ran away from the officer and was never seen again. There are a few problems with this theory, however. Let's start with a female LAPD officer walking a beat, alone, at night in one of the most dangerous parts of the city in 1947. It simply would not have occurred in a day and age when women were still not seen as equals. It was rare enough for a woman to be a beat cop, but those who were walking a beat always did so partnered with a male cop, almost never at night and certainly not alone. As the story mentions only the female cop as a witness, the tale is suspect from the start.

Elizabeth "Beth" Short had been living in San Diego for the last few months before she went missing. A male friend by the name of Robert Manley went down to pick Beth up and bring her to Los Angeles; Beth told him that her sister was picking her up at the Biltmore to take her back to Chicago and a new life. Manley, whose life was all but ruined by this case, told police that he did indeed drop her off at the Biltmore and that was the last time he saw her. It seems odd that a twenty-two-year-old woman who had hardly ever been to downtown Los Angeles would walk to the seediest part of town, alone, to go to a bar she had most likely never been to.

It is said by the first person to tell this tale that the bar at the Hotel Cecil was one of Elizabeth Short's favorite hangouts. The problem with this is that after the humiliation of being arrested for underage drinking and sent back home to the East Coast, Elizabeth never really drank again. She might, on very rare occasions, have a drink during social events, but even then, she would nurse one drink for the whole evening. After Beth returned to California, she moved into the house of Mark Hanson, then manager of the Florentine Club in Hollywood, and lived there with Ann Toth. The house was nowhere near downtown Los Angeles, and as Short didn't drink, there was no reason for her to go anywhere near Skid Row. Toth said of Short, "Betty could not stand up to trouble....She was skeptical of people." In other words, she wasn't the type to seek out the worst area in the entire city as a place to frequently hang out. When Beth did leave Hollywood, it was to go to Long Beach, California, to spend time and stay with her old boyfriend, Joseph Fickling. It was during this time that reporters, after talking with witnesses at the café in Long Beach where Short used to eat, came up with the nickname Black Dahlia. By the time this urban legend about the Black Dahlia's connection to the Cecil arose, the hotel was already known as a cursed and troubled place, and including it in a book about the Black Dahlia would have brought extra intrigue and drama to any historical fiction account of the mysterious murder.

One good thing happened at the Hotel Cecil in the beginning of the 1940s. Because of the prostitution, drug use and heavy drinking going on at the hotel and the huge number of bars surrounding it, Alcoholics Anonymous, which was created in 1935, decided to host its first meetings in Los Angeles at the hotel. But even after a change in management, extensive improvements and AA meetings to help those living on Skid Row, the darkness surrounding the hotel continued. Those living at the hotel still died from alcohol poisoning, drugs and causes that folks began attributing to the "curse"—like a café manager who was living at the hotel being shot during a gun battle with a bartender who had been his childhood best friend. Add this to the other deaths both in and outside the hotel involving its residents, and its reputation for evil grew.

The 1950s was a slow time for what many now called the Curse of the Cecil Hotel. Only one suicide seems to have occurred at the hotel during this time, that of Helen Gurnee, a fifty-five-year-old stationery firm employee from San Diego. Gurnee registered under the name of Margaret Brown of Denver and promptly threw herself out of her seventh-floor window. Gurnee landed on the hotel's marquee, and what the newspapers reported were "hundreds of spectators gathered" to watch firemen and ambulance attendants lower her body. It was shortly after Helen Gurnee's suicide that the long-term residents of the Hotel Cecil began calling the building "The Suicide."

It would seem that the lull of the 1950s was so that the supposed curse could save up for the horrors of the 1960s. On February 11, 1962, Julia Moore jumped from her eighth-floor window, her body landing on the second-floor railing. All Moore left behind was a bus ticket, fifty-nine cents and a bankbook showing a balance of $1,800. That same year, on October 12, perhaps the most infamous suicide the hotel has known occurred when Pauline Otton jumped out of her ninth-floor window and landed on the street below. What makes this suicide so unusual is the fact that not only did Otton commit suicide, but she also committed murder. Main Street in Los Angeles is and was a very busy street, with folks constantly walking along the sidewalks of Skid Row. When Otton decided to kill herself and jumped from the window of the Cecil, she never took that into consideration. As a result, when her body hit the walkway below the hotel, she landed on sixty-five-year-old transient George Giannini, killing them both instantly. When police arrived at the scene, they originally thought that it was a double suicide—until they noticed that Giannini was still wearing his shoes. They said his shoes would have fallen off in the long drop from the building and realized that he was simply an innocent victim of Otton. As reported in the *Desert Sun* on October 13, 1962, "Mrs. Pauline Otton, 27, Los Angeles, wrote a suicide note to her husband then leaped nine stories from the Cecil Hotel. George Giannini, 65, a transient, was struck by Mrs. Otton's hurtling body. Coroner's deputies said both were dead at the scene Friday night."

The 1960s also saw the unsolved murder of a beloved resident of the Cecil, Pauline Osgood, known by the nickname Pigeon Goldie. Osgood garnered this nickname due to her love for the pigeons in nearby Pershing Square, which she would feed every day. Goldie, a retired telephone operator living at the Hotel Cecil, was discovered in her room by a hotel employee who was distributing phone books. The scene that the worker found was gruesome: Osgood's body was found next to the LA Dodgers baseball cap she always wore and a bag of birdseed ready for her next trip to Pershing Square. Pidgeon Golding, age sixty, had been raped, strangled and then stabbed multiple times before the killer simply left her there. The killer was never found, and no one had heard a thing, not even those in the adjoining rooms. Goldie's became another case that furthered the growing rumors of paranormal involvement that were now being spread.

The 1970s were another period during which the Cecil may have been storing up its energy for the coming of the 1980s. Only one death of note occurred during the '70s, and no one is sure if it was a suicide or something more sinister. A woman who registered under the alias Alison Lowell stayed at the hotel for four days before she seemingly fell from the window of her room, 327, and was found dead on the second-floor roof of the hotel. But as low as the death rate was in the 1970s, the 1980s would see two of the evilest men in history walk through the lobby of the Hotel Cecil: Richard Ramirez and Jack Unterweger.

Richard Ramirez was one of the most vile and evil men ever to have walked this Earth. Many believe that his childhood is to blame for his violent and sadistic behavior, and it may have contributed to it, but even without those influences, the man was downright evil. He was first arrested at the age of seventeen for possession while still living in Texas, where he grew up, but once released from jail, he moved to California, quickly became addicted to cocaine, began a career in burglary and became infatuated with satanism—not the religion of satanism but the occult devotion to Satan himself, with all the evils and practices that came with it. By the time Ramirez walked through the doors of the Hotel Cecil, he had been arrested twice for auto theft. The Cecil at that time was a rundown flophouse filled with lost souls, drug addicts, pimps, dealers and all types from the criminal element of LA. It was so bad that no one noticed Ramirez's neglect of personal hygiene. He stank, his teeth were rotting, his hair was matted—and he fit right in with the rest of those living at the hotel.

It was in April 1984 that Ramirez would graduate from simple robbery to rape, torture and murder. That month, a nine-year-old child was found raped and murdered in San Francisco; however, no one was ever arrested, and no suspects were ever found. That is, until 2009, when DNA samples from Ramirez were found to match those taken at the crime scene. Ramirez was never charged with the killing of this child. Two months after the discovery of the nine-year-old, on June 28, 1984, Jennie Vincow was found raped, stabbed and murdered in what authorities called a violent home invasion and robbery. This was the first murder attributed to Ramirez, but it certainly would not be the last. It took him nine months to strike again, but once he did, there was no stopping him.

Hotel Hayward was the Hotel Cecil's main competitor. *From the New York Public Library, https://digitalcollections.nypl.org/items/510d47d9-9e6d-a3d9-e040-e00a18064a99.*

On March 17, 1985, Ramirez attacked Maria Hernandez in her San Fernando Valley home. Maria managed to escape, but her roommate, Dayle Okazaki was killed. That same evening, Ramirez shot and killed Tsai-Lian Yu, and the media began calling Ramirez the "Valley Intruder." More attacks followed in the coming months, with Ramirez using the same pattern in his murder spree: any male in the home would be shot, then the wife or girlfriend would be brutally raped and stabbed to death, after which Ramirez would rob the home of any valuables. In one particularly sick and violent act, Ramirez gouged out victim Maxine Zazzara's eyes and took them as souvenirs. After this, Ramirez went on a killing spree, committing over a dozen murders. At many of the crime scenes, it was found that Ramirez had performed a satanic ritual, seemingly to gain the favor of Satan with his heinous acts. However vicious Ramirez was, there were a few victims who managed to escape his clutches, and these folks helped the LAPD, which had set up a taskforce to catch the killer, produce a drawing of what he looked like. These sketches were put out all over the city and in the media, forcing Ramirez to flee Los Angeles for San Francisco.

Once up north, Ramirez killed again, twice. As he did not change his pattern and still performed his rituals, the San Francisco Police Department knew who they were looking for, and the media, now that Ramirez had left the Valley, began calling him the "Night Stalker." Ramirez, knowing he wasn't safe in either San Francisco or LA, decided to head back to the city, and hotel, he felt comfortable in and once again began committing crimes. This time, with his picture posted everywhere, there was nowhere for him to hide. On August 31, 1985, while trying to carjack a car in East LA, Ramirez was caught by a group of residents, beaten badly and held until police arrived to take him into custody. No charges were brought against or admonishments given to this group of concerned citizens. Finally, the reign of terror brought by this evil monster had come to an end. Ramirez was given the death sentence, which was later commuted to life in prison with no possibility of parole. He died from cancer while in prison in 2013. I have no doubt he now resides in a very warm climate.

It is said that satanic rituals were performed many times at the Hotel Cecil and that is why the hotel has such a dark past. There has never been any evidence that such rituals were ever performed at the Cecil; history itself does not even support Ramirez having performed them. It is this author's belief that Ramirez's devotion to satanism and the rituals he performed at the murder scenes led to this urban legend. One odd thing about Ramirez and the Hotel Cecil is the fact that Ramirez would dump his bloody clothes in the dumpster outside of the hotel and walk through the hotel to his fourteenth-floor room wearing only his boxers or, sometimes, naked while covered in blood and not a single person took notice, not even the staff. It is a strange ending to a horrendous chapter in the life of the Cecil.

Ramirez was not the only serial killer to call the Hotel Cecil home. Jack Unterweger also lived at the hotel after fleeing his native Austria to avoid going back to prison for life. Unterweger was another man whose childhood many blame for his evil nature. Unterweger was convicted of murdering a prostitute, Margaret Schaefer, in 1976. He was sentenced to life in prison and would spend the rest of his life there—that is, until luminaries, authors and news celebrities took up his cause as a "reformed man." Unterweger learned to read and write while in prison, and when he wrote a best-selling book about his life and guilt (mostly blaming his prostitute mother for giving him up) "intellectuals" around Germany and Austria began calling for him to be released as he was obviously reformed. They eventually won out, and Jack Unterweger was released—and became an instant celebrity. He would give interviews, talks and readings from his works, and many took inspiration from what he talked about. He had become what he always wanted to be: famous.

Everything was going great for Unterweger until a body was found in the woods near his home. Eventually, the bodies of at least nine missing prostitutes were found, and they all appeared to have been killed in the same way, the trademark way Jack Unterweger was known to kill. They were strangled with their own bras, using a knot that would allow the victim to be on the brink of death, only to be instantly brought back by releasing the knot. Unterweger, knowing that the law was about to catch up to him, fled to Los Angeles. Once he arrived in LA, Unterweger made folks believe he was on an assignment to write a piece about the "terrible conditions suffered by American prostitutes." So convincing was Unterweger that the LAPD gave him an official ride-along. Unterweger decided that the Hotel Cecil would be the best place to continue his murderous ways. Many believe that Unterweger chose the Hotel Cecil to honor Richard Ramirez. This may be true, but there has never been a mention of Ramirez in any of Unterweger's writings, talks or speeches—nothing to say that he even knew who Ramirez was, let alone admired him. It is more likely that Unterweger chose the Cecil due to its location in the heart of Skid Row and its prostitutes.

Whatever reason Jack Unterweger had for staying at the Hotel Cecil, it was here that he tortured and murdered three local prostitutes. He tortured the three girls in the same way he did his other victims, by tying his special knot in their bra straps and repeatedly choking them to the brink of death, reviving them and repeating the torture until he became bored and allowed them to die. After the LAPD noticed the similarities between the three girls killed in LA and those in Austria, they set their sights on Unterweger and realized that the murders in LA coincided with his arrival. Once Unterweger learned that he was being sought by Austrian authorities and LAPD was on to him, he fled to Switzerland, then Paris and finally to Miami. It was here that the FBI set a trap for him by claiming to be from *Success* magazine and wanting to pay him $10,000 for an interview. Unterweger, always one for the spotlight, agreed to the interview and was apprehended by U.S. marshals on his arrival at the "studio." Unterweger was eventually extradited back to Austria, convicted and sentenced again to life in prison without parole. The very first night Jack Unterweger spent behind bars, he used the string from his own prison jumpsuit to hang himself. One Austrian politician quipped the following day that it was "Unterweger's best murder."

Ramirez in the 1980s and Jack Unterweger in the 1990s seemed to sum up what a lot of folks call the "evil of the Cecil." Yes, both of these men can and should be considered evil. It is understandable that, after the sheer amount of horror that had taken place at the Hotel Cecil over the years it had been in business, people would believe that the place was possessed, possibly by demonic forces. But the Cecil wasn't finished with its high strangeness and

Although the Hotel Cecil is situated on Skid Row, one can still find diners and decent food nearby, like this Cajun eatery next to the hotel.

deadly curse at the end of the century. No, the Hotel Cecil still had at least one more horror to inflict on the unsuspecting City of Angels.

The most well-known event to ever occur at the Hotel Cecil was the disappearance of Canadian Elisa Lam in 2013. For nineteen days, this innocent yet troubled young woman made international headlines and became an Internet sensation, with thousands of folks acting as an ad hoc investigative team and millions around the world hoping and praying that Elisa would be found alive and well. Elisa was found, but the way she was discovered is stomach-churning, and although her death was officially declared accidental, many believe that a massive cover-up took place and that Elisa Lam was actually murdered. This is due to the fact that although the police released elevator security footage of Lam in the hopes of someone having seen her before she went missing at the Cecil, it later came to light that the video footage had been altered before it was released.

The elevator security footage shows Lam performing bizarre movements and mannerisms and possibly attempting to hide from someone in the hallway outside the elevator. At one point—and this was clearly pointed out in the Netflix documentary *Crime Scene: The Vanishing at the Cecil Hotel*—

the toe of a person's shoe can be seen in one of the frames before moving away, past Elisa. In the documentary, the police justify altering of the footage by claiming that, yes, they did slow down the video in the hopes someone could identify Elisa. This is a strange statement, considering they had already identified her and told viewers who they were seeing. Also, they admitted to altering the video's timestamp so folks wouldn't know the exact time the video was captured. This statement is contrary to their stated hope that someone would have seen her at the time the video was recorded. Thirdly, it is clear that a section of the video was cut, as the elevator door "jumps" about six inches instead of sliding shut as normal. The LAPD claimed that it was cut so folks didn't see something that the police wanted to keep under wraps. This is a bit easier to understand, but if there was someone there they didn't want folks to see or something Elisa did that they didn't want witnessed, why not release all the details in the documentary after the case was solved?

The documentary also highlights the fact that the police originally stated the lid of the water tank where Elisa's body was finally discovered was closed yet later said it was found open. For nineteen days, they never corrected themselves, allowing folks to believe a murderer was on the loose in LA. The police searched the roof, including the outbuilding that stood over the water tanks, yet never noticed that the lid was off the tank? Also, the maintenance man did not state whether the tank was found open or closed until the end of the documentary and then, in a departure from his normal way of confidently looking at the camera, stared down at the floor. This is similar to when former hotel manager (2007–2017) Amy Price, while discussing the video footage being altered, couldn't stop her eyes from blinking in rapid succession—the only time this happened during her interviews in the documentary. Both of these behaviors are a body language tell that someone is lying.

Elisa Lam was found nineteen days after she went missing due to those living and staying at the hotel complaining about low water pressure and the water having a strange brown color and tasting "funny" and sour. The complaints prompted the hotel to send its maintenance manager to investigate what the problem might be. Going up to the roof, he peered into the very tank that Elisa Lam was floating in and immediately told manager Price, who called the LAPD.

Another strange occurrence has to do with Lam's autopsy report. The report was delayed months, and when released, it claimed the cause of Lam's death was "accidental drowning." What is odd about the report is that no liquid was found in Elisa Lam's lungs, no foam in her airways and no fluids of any kind to indicate she had actually drowned. Others believe that Lam was used by the Canadian government, in conjunction with the United States, to develop a biological weapon. The reason for this had to do with the fact that Lam went to the University of British Columbia, which had a large, well-respected tuberculosis lab and that just three days after Lam's body was found, TB began spreading through the Skid Row population and the Hotel Cecil. Coupled with the fact that the new test for TB that had just been released was called the Lam-Elisa test, many say that she was patient zero and was killed to cover up the fact that TB was used to reduce the homeless population in LA. With all the oddness involved with this case, it is no wonder folks believe there was some sort of cover-up—or that the Cecil is one of the most haunted hotels to ever receive guests.

The Hotel Cecil has become known as the "most haunted hotel in history." This seems to go against what the hotel staff has said going back the eight or more years I have been going there as an investigator to speak with employees. Granted, the hotel had been trying to get away from this reputation, but I have found that it is almost impossible to get 100 percent of employees not to talk about ghostly happenings in their place of work. If, as the hotel's Facebook page now indicates, it is seriously haunted, why are there virtually no stories regarding hauntings at the hotel, even on social media? It seems that the only evidence we have comes from a TV show and a TikTok influencer who said he lived across the street from the hotel. With fourteen million followers and a bank account to match, it seems unlikely that he would choose to live in a Skid Row apartment—but of course, I could be wrong.

The Hotel Cecil has been trying to change its image for years and the Stay on Main, a hotel within a hotel, was a way for them to do this. However, after Elisa Lam became a part of the Cecil's horrific history, the Stay on Main, where she was staying, became just another victim of the curse of the Hotel Cecil. Amy Price, the former manager of the hotel, said in an interview for *Esquire* (February 10, 2021), "I believe in ghosts but I don't think they run the show over there." She went on to say that in her ten years working there, she never had a paranormal experience, never saw a ghost and never once thought about it. Price did say that while she was working there, at least eighty people died at the Cecil.

While researching ghost stories about the hotel, I could not find a single ghost story other than two social media accounts. Now, the TikTok influencer did say that while he was living across the street from the Cecil, he witnessed

Once a grand hotel, the Cecil is now run-down and used for Section 8 housing.

a woman "standing in the window of one of the hotel rooms" and that when he called out to her, she didn't respond. He called 911, thinking the woman was about to jump, but paramedics discovered she was just filming something. After he put his footage on TikTok, his followers began claiming the woman didn't look real, that she was obviously the ghost of a woman who had killed herself and so on. As for the TV show, I won't go into what they eventually "found."

For anyone interested in the Elisa Lam case, the Netflix documentary is fantastic and highly recommended. The documentary explains away the reports of a spirit or demon keeping the elevator door from closing and the elevator from moving. In the row of buttons that Lam presses during her bipolar episode was the "elevator hold" button, on the bottom. This button, when pressed, keeps the elevator stationary and the door open for two minutes; Lam presses this button at least two times. The video also shows what floor Lam was on during this episode. In the center of the top row of buttons is the button for the fourteenth floor. As Lam presses each button, they light up, indicating the elevator will travel to that floor; however, the top button, after being pressed, goes dark, indicating that Elisa Lam was already on the fourteenth floor.

The Hotel Cecil was designed and built to be a luxury hotel in the heart of downtown Los Angeles, a place for the wealthy and the middle class to come and enjoy all the amenities it had to offer, but fate had other plans. What the Hotel Cecil became was a place for mischief, mayhem, horror and evil. Today, the hotel is no longer open to guests but has become a low-income housing establishment catering to the homeless and lost souls of Skid Row. Is it haunted? Given the amount of death associated with the hotel over the years, the answer is most likely yes. Is it filled with demonic entities causing the hotel to murder its own guests? Most likely no. Is it cursed? As I stated in the beginning of this chapter, I don't believe in curses—or do I now?

CHAPTER 7
THE MILLENNIUM BILTMORE HOTEL

Right in the heart of downtown Los Angeles stands one of the grandest hotels ever built in the City of Angels. Even though it has a direct Hollywood connection (it is said that Oscar was born in one of the ballrooms), not many folks think about "Oscar" walking through the Biltmore's doors or strolling through its ornate interior and lavish appointments. The history of this legendary hotel mirrors that of Los Angeles: its meteoric rise, its slow decline into obscurity and its rise from the ashes parallel Los Angeles' in many ways. History almost bleeds from the walls of the hotel—and with its Hollywood roots, its association with Route 66 and its connection to one of the most mysterious and gruesome unsolved murders in the annals of law enforcement, it shouldn't come as a surprise that the Millennium Biltmore is also one of the most haunted hotels in the entire city.

Opened on October 1, 1923, the Biltmore Hotel was constructed with the extremely rich in mind. With its grandiose luxury and lavish appointments throughout, the hotel was meant to bring the movers and shakers to Los Angeles and to show that the City of Angels was growing up and coming of age in what was becoming known as the entertainment capital of the world: Hollywood, with its studios and movie stars close at hand, along with the business district in the heart of Los Angeles. The Biltmore, just off Pershing Square and close to the terminus of Route 66, would become the obvious choice to stay for all the elite coming to town. It was designed in the Art Deco style of the day, and the owners spared no expense with either the

The Biltmore Hotel became the place to be for celebrities, politicians and mobsters.

exterior architecture or the interior appointments. Anyone checking in at the luxuriant and overstated lobby got the feeling they had just walked into one of the grand palaces of Europe rather than a hotel in the once-sleepy city of Los Angeles. The mastermind who created the feeling of royalty was Italian artist Giovanni Battista Smeraldi. Smeraldi was known for designing the Blue Room at the White House and many of the interiors in the Vatican. He had once been compared to Michelangelo and his work described as "Michelangelo-esque."

It didn't take long for Hollywood to notice this posh venue, and the day after the Biltmore opened, the hotel hosted a gala event with more than three thousand celebrities and Hollywood executives in attendance. Clark Gable, Myrna Loy, Mary Pickford, Jack Warner and Cecil B. DeMille were all in attendance, along with many of the country's rich and famous. Guests were treated to a seven-course meal, drinks, dancing and a symphony, replete with singing canaries. The celebration was a complete success, and Hollywood was suitably impressed. The Biltmore hotel became the place for Hollywood's elite to party and hold meetings, and it was here, in May 1927, that the Academy of Motion Picture Arts was founded in the hotel's Crystal Ballroom. The Academy Awards were held in the Biltmore in 1931, from 1935 to 1939 and from 1941 to 1942. It is also rumored that production designer Cedric Gibbons drew the first sketch of the Oscar award on one of the hotel's linen napkins. In 1977, Bob Hope hosted the fiftieth anniversary banquet for the awards in the Biltmore Bowl Room, the same room where the Academy Awards were held all those many years earlier.

Politicians, gamblers and mobsters all frequented the speakeasy that was established at the hotel shortly after Prohibition was enacted. When the sale and consumption of alcohol was made illegal with the passage of the Eighteenth Amendment, the Gold Room, which is adjacent to Olive Street, was converted into a speakeasy, a very proper and upscale one for the times. As respectable as the Gold Room was, it was still dealing with something that was illegal within the United States; as such, certain villainous personalities came to dance and drink the night away in opulence. It is said that Al Capone was a frequent guest of the Biltmore speakeasy. Since the same politicians who helped enact Prohibition came to the Biltmore to ignore it—along with the many gamblers (gambling was also illegal in Los Angeles) and gangsters in attendance—a secret door leading from the Gold Room out onto Olive Street was installed for those in need of a quick getaway, and the Gold Room quickly became the premier place for nightlife in Los Angeles among the wealthy. When Prohibition was repealed, the Biltmore was still the place

Young women selling hats supporting Senator John F. Kennedy outside the Biltmore Hotel during the Democratic National Convention, Los Angeles, California, July 1960. *Leffler, Warren K, photographer, via Library of Congress.*

to go, and it is said that Benjamin "Bugsy" Siegel frequented the hotel to wine and dine union bosses, mob moneymen and investors for his Las Vegas Casino. Today, the door leading to Olive Street is still there but now leads to a storage area as the outer door has been bricked over.

During World War II, the hotel housed military personnel, both those arriving from the war zone and those about to be shipped out. The second floor was used for these soldiers, and those lucky enough to stay there found the contrast of life in combat or training compared to life at the swanky Biltmore Hotel striking; in other words, they thoroughly enjoyed their stay. During the war, the USO also set up in the hotel, hosting charity events and war bond drives and helping with anything needed for the war effort. During the 1950s, when folks from all walks of life began to realize their newfound freedom on the road, travelers came to the Biltmore to celebrate in style the dawning of the new car culture emerging within the United States. Then, in 1960, Camelot had its beginnings as the Democratic National Convention was held at the Biltmore Hotel, nominating John F. Kennedy as candidate for president of the United States. As people watched Kennedy accept the nomination, it seemed as if hope for a bright new future was arising in the United States and nothing could stop it. That may have been so, but the fortunes of the Biltmore Hotel were in decline, but the hotel wasn't aware of this at the time.

By the end of the 1960s, Los Angeles had become a shell of its former self. Like most big cities in the country, it began to see an influx of the homeless. Shopping was moving to areas such as Beverley Hills with its high-end stores and name-brand Hollywood labels, and nearby beach communities were building tourist areas with gift shops right off the sand or "pleasure" piers that catered to all things beach culture. As the city began to decline, a lawless element began to grow, and gang activity was on the rise. As the city's vibrancy waned, the Biltmore slowly began to decline and was almost converted into a low-income retirement building just like others in the area. Luckily, before this could happen, an architecture firm, Ridgeway LTD, purchased the building in 1976 with the idea of restoring it to its original prominence. After an investment of about $250 million, the hotel did have a revival; however, it wasn't until the Millennium & Copthorne Group purchased the hotel in 2000 that the Biltmore saw its true resurgence. Today, the Millennium Biltmore Hotel is honored as an elite member of the Historic Hotels of America and once again has become one of Hollywood's "go-to" hotels.

The Biltmore Hotel prospered through the war years of the 1940s, Korea and Vietnam. It was witness to both Los Angeles riots and had to deal with gangsters, moonshiners, royalty and statesmen who all passed through, including Harry Truman, JFK, LBJ, Gerald Ford, Jimmy Carter, Ronald Reagan and Bill Clinton. Celebrities and movie stars such as Joan Crawford, Dolores Del Rio, Jimmy Stewart, Clark Gable, Claudette Colbert and Ginger Rodgers were frequent guests at the hotel, and fashion icons like Peggy Hamilton, Hedda Hopper and Versace have all stayed at the Biltmore. One other mysterious media magnet has also been known to walk the halls of the Millennium Biltmore, not because she was a socialite or Hollywood starlet but because the Biltmore was the last place this pretty young woman was seen alive, and in one piece. You see, the Millennium Biltmore is said to be one of the most haunted hotels in Los Angeles.

On January 15, 1947, Betty Bersinger walked down Norton Avenue in her Leimert Park neighborhood to pick up her husband's shoes. As she strolled along, she pondered how the empty lots along the street had become a dumping ground for people to leave their trash and old household items they no longer needed and how it was all becoming an eyesore. She noticed that someone had dumped a broken storefront mannequin in one of the lots and cursed whoever had done it. She spotted it right off because it was so white and looked very lifelike, even though it was obviously broken into two pieces. As she got closer, she realized that what she had taken for a mannequin was in fact the body of a young woman, and she quickly backed away so her young daughter, who was in a stroller, wouldn't see what was lying in the tall grass.

What Betty Bersinger found that morning was the mutilated nude body of Elizabeth Short. She had been cut in half at the navel, and chunks of flesh had been cut out of her abdomen. Bersinger also noticed that the woman's left leg and one of her breasts had been mutilated. Bersinger was appalled that the young woman had been positioned in what she and investigators assumed was the killer's attempt at a seductive pose. The woman's blue eyes were open, and her legs had been spread in a sexually suggestive position, with the arms of her torso—which was found a foot away from her lower half—raised over her head, elbows slightly bent. Her face had been cut from the sides of her mouth to her ears in an attempt to give her a permanent smile in death, à la the Joker. Perhaps the strangest thing about the naked corpse was that the killer had drained it of blood and thoroughly washed the body. What Betty Bersinger found that day would become one of the most famous unsolved murders in history: the case of the Black Dahlia.

Elizabeth Short was last seen heading up the stairs toward the elevator at the Biltmore Hotel. She had been dropped off there by a male friend, Robert "Red" Manley, so she could wait for her sister to come pick her up and take her back to Chicago. Elizabeth would never be seen alive again. There is some speculation that Short met family friend and prominent surgeon Walter Alonzo Bailey, whose office was around the corner from the Biltmore, and that he, in an Alzheimer's-fueled rage, murdered her. Unfortunately, we will never truly know who killed Elizabeth or why, but what we do know is that she still enjoys time at the Biltmore Hotel. (For more in-depth information regarding Elizabeth Short's life and death, please look for my book *Hollywood Obscura*.)

Perhaps the most dramatic sighting of the Black Dahlia comes to us from a man by the name of James Moore. Moore was staying at the Biltmore and, after a long day, headed upstairs to his room. He waited patiently for the elevator to come down to the lobby, and when the doors opened, he noticed a very pretty young woman had remained in the elevator. His eyes were drawn to her as she was dressed all in black and had very pale skin. She didn't speak to him but remained still, although she did glance in his direction a couple of times. As he pressed the button for his floor, he noticed

Elizabeth Short was last seen alive ascending these stairs.

that the panel was already lit up for the elevator to stop on the sixth floor, so when the doors opened on the sixth floor and the woman didn't move, he casually spoke to tell her that they had reached her floor. She again glanced toward him and then slowly walked out of the elevator. As the doors were closing, she turned back to him and, with a look he later described as a plea for help, started to get back into the elevator. The doors shut before she could reenter, and even though Moore frantically pushed the button, the door slid shut before reopening. As the elevator slowly opened, Moore exited the elevator to see if the young woman needed help, but she was nowhere to be seen. He searched the corridors near the elevator but couldn't find her anywhere. It had taken only a few moments for the doors to reopen, and in that time, the woman had completely vanished.

A couple of days after Moore saw the pretty young woman on the elevator, he was browsing through a local bookstore near the hotel and came across a book on true crimes and unsolved murders in Los Angeles. Moore picked up the book and began thumbing through it. He stood dumbfounded as a page opened that had a picture of the beautiful woman he had encountered in the elevator at the Biltmore. Her name was Elizabeth Short, and she had been murdered many years before he had even been born. Moore was shocked when he realized that he had taken an elevator ride with the ghost

The Black Dahlia is often seen riding these elevators.

of the Black Dahlia. He now knew why he couldn't get the sad, pretty young woman out of his head and why he would never be able to forget her.

Many folks have seen Elizabeth Short's spirit over the years, riding the elevator up to the sixth floor. Each time she is seen it is the same: she rides the lift in silence, occasionally glancing at the others in the elevator, and steps out of the lift as it reaches her floor. She always vanishes from sight before anyone else can get out or peek around the doors. Many believe that the Black Dahlia must have been brutally murdered in a room on the sixth floor. Unfortunately, we may never know the truth unless Elizabeth herself decides to finally let us know what happened to her.

The Black Dahlia is by no means the only spirit to call the Millennium Biltmore home in the afterlife. The ninth floor is not always a restful place to stay as guests will often be woken up in the middle of the night by the sound of a child's laughter. The laughter sounds like that of a playful little girl. This child has been seen playing in the corridors, and folks who have heard her say it sounds like she is having the time of her life. Witnesses have said that even though the child disturbed their sleep, the sound of her giggles brought a smile to their face. There is a young boy who seems to be haunting the hotel as well. He has been seen often on the roof of the hotel, although no one has been able to figure out why the roof is so appealing to him. When the boy is seen, no facial features can be glimpsed; it is as if the child has no face. With no way to see his face, there is no place to begin research into who he might be.

As many servicemen came through and used the Biltmore as a resting place during and after World War II, and as many of those men were from small towns and rural areas and thus unused to the kind of luxury the Biltmore provided, it would seem that quite a few soldiers have decided to stay at the posh hotel after death. There have been numerous reports of ghostly soldiers walking through the old lobby in what is now the Rendezvous Court, an area that now serves breakfast, lunch and drinks. Employees have said that they are constantly having to answer questions about the many ghosts that are seen moving about and passing through. Another spirit often reported at the hotel is that of a nurse who is seen on the second floor. As this is the floor where the hotel housed returning servicemen, it is assumed that she may have been a returning combat nurse.

The Millennium Biltmore Hotel is so haunted that you can even find reviews mentioning the ghosts on TripAdvisor. One reviewer, in March 2021, said the phone in their room kept ringing, but when they tried to answer, it gave them a dial tone. They would hang the phone up, turn around—and the phone would ring again. This same guest said that when

It is here that both guests and employees alike hear disembodied voices and sounds of partying and feel as if they are being watched from the shadows.

trying to go to sleep, they kept having the sensation of a feather brushing across their face, and strange dreams kept creeping into their head as they tried to sleep. Another review stated that no matter where the writer was in the lobby or other public areas, they would feel as if they were being watched by unseen figures. They said that other guests they spoke with told them they had the same feeling. Both employees and guests say that they will often hear the sounds of a party going on, even though there are no gatherings or events going on at the Biltmore at that time and that they can see spirits watching them out of the corner of their eye, only to, when they look in that direction, find no one there. There have also been reports of sudden temperature drops followed by noises that can't be defined, knocks coming from empty rooms and even the sounds of conversations coming from rooms where no people are present.

The Millennium Biltmore Hotel has seen so much history over its lifespan that it has become almost a time capsule for the City of Los Angeles. It has seen the city rise and it has seen the city fall, and it was there when the city had its rebirth. The Biltmore Hotel has been through the same changes at the same time as Los Angeles and has come back stronger and more luxurious than ever. That history not only includes the brick and mortar of the building itself but also the spirits that still call the City of Angels and the Millennium Biltmore home today.

CHAPTER 8

LOS ANGELES LIZARD MEN

Lizard people have been reported all over the world for as long as the human race has been in existence. Even today, tales of these elusive iguanas spring up on a regular basis all over the globe. The New Jersey Gator Man; the Lizard-Man of Scape Ore Swamp in South Carolina; the Loveland, Ohio Frogmen; and the much-maligned Lizard Demon of West Virginia have all become part of American folklore. None of these, however, come close to the industrious Los Angeles Lizard Men.

Springing from a Hopi Indian myth, the lizard people of Los Angeles built an entire civilization along the West Coast of California and lived peacefully until a massive meteor storm destroyed what they had built. To protect themselves from future disasters of this type, the tribe built thirteen subterranean settlements along the Pacific Coast that could house their families, protect their heritage and allow them to live in safety.

The lizards were able to accomplish this feat by using a chemical solution that melted solid rock. It is said that the lizard people were so much smarter than humans that, by today's standards, a nine-year-old lizard child had the equivalent IQ and education of a college graduate.

Knowledge of the Los Angeles Lizard Men came to the general public in the 1930s when a mining engineer by the name of George Warren Shufelt convinced the LA City Council that there was an elaborate tunnel system under the streets of the city that contained a wealth of gold and other treasures just waiting for someone to find them. Shufelt said that Los Angeles would get half of everything he found in the lizard tunnels if they allowed him to excavate the ground over the tunnels. The city council agreed.

As it turns out, Shufelt had invented a "radio X-ray machine" just for this purpose. According to Shufelt, he found nineteen thousand square feet of tunnels with over nine thousand feet of floor space and sixteen places where gold was stored. He said the entire underground complex was shaped like a lizard with the "head" at Elysian Park and the tip of the "tail" where today's Central Library sits. According to the X-ray device, the gold chamber was situated under the Banning property at 518 North Hill Street, and so Shufelt occupied the land and dug a 350-foot shaft straight down looking for the treasure room. He dug in the area for just over a year but never found his treasure-filled pot of gold. Then, shortly after a *Los Angeles Times* article appeared, describing the city-authorized project in detail, all work stopped, Shufelt and his partners disappeared and the whole venture began to be seen as a great hoax perpetrated against the city by a clever con man.

Whether or not Shufelt was a delusional mining engineer convinced by a Hopi chief that the lizard treasure was real or a con man out to bilk one of the largest cities in the United States is up for debate, but in any case, there may be some validity to the story of the lost city of the lizards. Over the years since Shufelt and his cohorts gave up their excavations, tunnels have been mysteriously turning up under the streets of Los Angeles. To date, a full eleven miles of tunnels have been found, and it is believed that many more are awaiting discovery. One of the most well-known tunnels lies under city hall. This tunnel is wide enough to drive a car through and is said to have been used by criminals and moonshiners and, at one time, for transporting over $1 billion in cash. Another tunnel, now completely closed off to the public, was used to transport criminals from the jail facility to the Hall of Justice.

In 1954, a strange amulet was found in northern Los Angeles County near an old railroad tunnel that even today has scientists baffled. The artifact is silver, fused to a copper alloy base that is composed of over forty different types of metal. The front of the amulet depicts a full-bodied dragon, a type of lizard. The medallion itself is said to be thousands of years old. This type of metallurgy was not known in that period—or so we thought. It is believed that the lizard people were a highly intelligent race, and this type of science might well have been within their abilities. Could this amulet be proof that the lizards were here?

Most people believe that the Los Angeles Lizard Men have long been extinct. However, over the years, a few reports of these beings have come to light. Jacob Cohen worked in the Banning tunnels underneath downtown Los Angeles when he was young and spoke about encountering one of the lizard people while in the tunnels. Cohen said that there had been a cave-in and he had gone back into the tunnel looking for his uncle. He found quite a few bodies along with the body of his uncle and said that not only did they have injuries consistent with a cave-in but that some of them also had what looked like claw marks on their bodies. As Cohen stood staring at the dead men in front of him, he heard what sounded like something heavy being dragged across the tunnel floor. When he looked toward the sound, he saw something with shiny skin and fingers moving away down the tunnel. Cohen said he told the foreman and investigators what he had seen, but they dismissed his story as something from the mind of a frightened sixteen-year-old.

Another story comes from one of the many homeless people who inhabit the streets of Los Angeles. One night in the early 2000s, a man, who was known to the local police, wandered into the station and seemed "scared to even breathe," as one officer put it. The vagabond told police that he had been rummaging in a trash can near Union Station when he heard a noise coming from one of the nearby maintenance tunnels. He said it sounded like something scraping along the wall of the tunnel and that he heard a strange hissing sound. When he peeked into the maintenance tunnel, there, right in front of him, was an enormous lizard, standing up on its hind legs and staring at him with its yellow, slitted eyes. When the creature hissed at him, he turned and started to run, and the lizard man reached out and tripped him and took his shoes. The police, of course, laughed at the man, thinking he was probably drunk, high or perhaps just crazy—that is, until the homeless man showed them the deep scratches on his legs. The vagabond needed eight stitches on one leg and four on the other. When the cops asked the doctor what could have caused those kinds of scratches, the doctor told them that it looked like they were made by alligator claws. The police officers just looked at each other but didn't say a word.

There are those who believe that the lizard men are nothing more than the natural evolution of the dinosaurs. These reptiles were smart enough to have lived through the meteor blast and the ice age and have also remained hidden from us by way of their far superior intellect, developed over millennia. There are others who believe that the Lizard People are an alien race that have already taken the reins of power within our societies by becoming part of every royal bloodline and making sure that every elected official, including the United States president, are a part of the lizard/human hybrid race they have been developing for hundreds of years. Whatever the case may be, the Los Angeles Lizard Men not only seem to want to remain solitary, but they also seem to care little for the politics of those who live on the surface they may have once called home.

CHAPTER 9

DODGER STADIUM AND THE BATTLE OF CHAVEZ RAVINE

Anyone who follows Major League Baseball knows the Los Angeles Dodgers. From the Brooklyn Greys of 1883, through entering Major League Baseball as the Brooklyn Bridegrooms, changing their name to the Dodgers in 1911 and finally playing their first home game in Los Angeles at the Memorial Colosseum in 1958 before moving into their permanent home, Dodger Stadium—this franchise has played in thirty-seven playoff series and amassed seven championship seasons to become one of the winningest teams in Major League Baseball history. In Los Angeles alone, the Dodgers have a record of twenty-eight playoffs and six championships. The Dodgers fan base is one of the most devoted in baseball, and season tickets are hard to come by. With all the winning seasons, devoted Dodger Blue fanatics and billions of dollars in merchandise being sold yearly, one wonders how many fans also know about the cost in human suffering the Dodgers brought with them to the City of Angels or about the spirits that now call Dodger Stadium their home in the afterlife.

As this is a book about Los Angeles, I will not go into the history of the Dodger organization other than how it relates to the land where the stadium now resides, Chavez Ravine. The ravine was named after Julian Chavez, who, along with his brother Mario, came to El Pueblo de Los Angeles in the late 1830s. Julian became a city official and acquired eighty-three acres of land in 1844 in what at that time was called Stone Quarry Hills. Julian and Mario were ranchers by trade and figured that building their own ranch

Dodger Stadium, also sometimes called Chavez Ravine, Los Angeles, California. *Highsmith, Carol M, photographer, via Library of Congress.*

near the growing pueblo was a good business strategy. The significant clay deposits in the area used for the construction of the new city didn't hurt either. The entire area was made up of several ravines, including Sulphur, Solano, Cemetery and Reservoir Ravines. Not much is known about exactly what the Chavez brothers did with the land, but during the smallpox epidemics of 1850 and 1880, we know that a hospital for both Mexican American and Chinese American patients was set up in Chavez Ravine. This seemed to be a catalyst for folks to begin settling in the ravines of Stone Quarry Hills.

Three separate neighborhoods sprang up across Cemetery and Sulphur Ravines; these were named La Loma, Bishop and Palo Verde. Other homes were built along the ridges of the ravines, but these three communities became the main centers of what would become known as Chavez Ravine. The area was completely self-sufficient, with residents building their own homes, growing their own food and teaching in their own school, and it became a very tight-knit community in the middle of what was becoming an urban sprawl. The citizens of Los Angeles began calling Chavez Ravine a "poor man's Shangri-la."

Then, in 1913, Marshall Stimson, a lawyer and Los Angeles political figure, saw the need for families who were then living on the floodplain of the Los Angeles River to move to higher and safer ground, so he began offering old homes he owned in and near the Palo Verde neighborhood to those willing to repair them and make them livable.

Palo Verde was named for a tree that grew at the fork of Bishop's Road, the main road into the ravine. Bishop's Road intersected North Broadway, a commercial street that featured a rail line, the "Yellow Cars," making it easy to begin bringing in goods to the three ravine neighborhoods. This is one of the reasons Stimson had bought up many of the lots in the Palo Verde area. Stimson, still a businessman, made money on the sales and rentals but also developed a good rapport with the community and a reputation for leniency and fairness among his tenants. Stimson managed to relocate 250 Mexican American families from the river into Chavez Ravine, but even with the population growth, the sense of small-town living still permeated the three neighborhoods, and the residents still grew their food, raised their animals and lived happily in the ravine. By 1926, Chavez Ravine had its own grocery store, a school, a small network of markets and a church. It was no different than any other neighborhood in Los Angeles. That same year, the folks living there, having suffered through years of blasting, formed a committee to petition the city council to close down the brick manufacturers still operating in their area. In a unanimous decision in August 1926, the council zoned Chavez Ravine for residential use only and passed an ordinance prohibiting blasting of any kind. The city had finally recognized the area as an official part of the city.

Throughout the late 1920s and into the '30s, and without city services such as a reliable sewage system or street paving and maintenance, Chavez Ravine grew and flourished, even when the Great Depression gripped the country and the world. The Depression may not have been too much of a problem for the neighborhood; however, in the mid- to late 1930s, the federal government, under the leadership of FDR, created the New Deal agencies. Two of these, the Home Owners' Loan Corporation (HOLC) and the Federal Housing Administration (FHA), began providing low-interest private mortgages with only small down payments required so that working-class Americans could own their own homes. To facilitate these loans and to help keep defaults at a minimum, the loans were targeted through what the feds called a "neighborhood risk" system. They directed city governments to assess potential neighborhoods within the city through the City Survey Program. So, beginning in 1935, the City of LA began assigning investment grades to areas, corresponding to their potential eligibility to receive federally insured mortgages and insurance. Often, in the early twentieth century, White neighborhoods were given priority for such programs, while minority areas were either overlooked or branded as slums. Chavez Ravine was no different. Due to the fact that most of the homes and structures there were

Eight dollars was a tidy sum for a ramshackle abode that may or may not have had running water or a toilet. *From the New York Public Library.*

hand built and city services, even at this time, were lacking, Los Angeles and the federal government identified the neighborhood as "blighted."

Once the label of "blighted community" was in place, it had a direct effect on the area by keeping funds from Chavez Ravine residents to help repair their housing or to effectively expand the neighborhood. Another unfortunate result of the designation was that it put Chavez Ravine on the radar of the city's redevelopment department. This, along with the HOLC assessment, put the neighborhood on a priority list for demolition. Luckily, in 1937, regional boosters were planning the Pacific Mercado, an international exposition to celebrate the four hundredth anniversary of Cabrillo's voyage along California's coast, and the site they picked for this celebration was Chavez Ravine. The following year, as plans moved forward for the exposition, the city's engineering department proposed a new limited-access highway (similar to the Arroyo Parkway, which was still under construction) that would cut the driving time from downtown LA to the San Fernando Valley. That same year, the U.S. Navy announced that it was going to build a new $1 million armory in Chavez Ravine. With the navy's announcement, the boosters' plans were dashed, and a grand expo was never seen. The only plan that would go forward, backed by FDR's Works Progress Administration (WPA), would be the navy's new armory. However, all these plans helped keep Chavez Ravine from the wrecking ball.

When the United States was thrust into World War II in December 1941, Chavez Ravine was put on the back burner. Many of the residents of this Mexican American community joined up to fight for their country, and many came back heroes. Unfortunately, heroism is fleeting, and once the war was over, Los Angeles once again revisited the "blight" of Chavez Ravine. Even though the public works proposals had kept Chavez Ravine intact, now the city began looking to its lands for use in the name of the "public good." By 1949, the city had decided that the homes in Chavez Ravine should be torn down and the area used for "urban renewal." Bolstered by the federal Housing Act of 1949, Democrat mayor Fletcher Bowron and his allies on the city council sought to remove residents from Chavez Ravine to begin the process. On the other side was the real estate lobby, backed by the chamber of commerce and Norman Chandler, publisher of the *Los Angeles Times*, who wanted urban renewal but in the service of commercial interests. Either way you look at it, neither side had the interests of the Chavez Ravine residents in mind.

On July 24, 1950, the Los Angeles City Housing Authority (CHA), on behalf of the FHA, who would be given ownership of the land, informed Chavez Ravine's residents of the plans to replace their community with a public housing project they didn't want. At the time the announcement was made, there were approximately 1,200 families living in the three individual neighborhoods of Palo Verde, Bishop and La Loma. They were all informed that they would have to move from their homes and the community they had built over the years. The new development would include thirteen high-density high-rise apartment buildings and a complex of churches, shops, schools and recreational facilities, all under the name Elysian Park Heights. Those living in the ravine were told that they would have first choice of the new dwellings and would be given fair recompense for the sale of their homes and land. City officials assumed that the "impoverished slum

Dodger Stadium is sometimes referred to as Chavez Ravine, but that name is now found only on street signs.

dwellers" would welcome what they believed would be a clear improvement in living conditions. This short-sighted idea was completely wrong and placed Chavez Ravine on a collision course with the City of Los Angeles.

The word *fair* is subjective—and no more so than when dealing with a government agency. As the CHA began buying up the homes in December 1950, it became clear that *fair*, to Los Angeles, meant below-market cash offers. Only a small group of families accepted what the city offered outright, but many noticed the disparity between the offers for homes in Chavez Ravine and housing prices in other areas of the city. Many of those who accepted the low-bid offers were immediately sent into newfound poverty and debt. When some residents refused to sell, the city responded by claiming that those families whose main wage-earners were undocumented were ineligible for public housing and by making ever lower offers to those who refused to sell. Many folks, scared that the offers would stop altogether, accepted the extremely low offers, and the ones who still held out were threatened with having their homes condemned and their power shut off and with the use of eminent domain.

As the threats by the LA City Council continued, the folks who remained in Chavez Ravine, Christine Sterling among them, organized a protest outside Mayor Bowron's office in 1951, and in April that year, residents packed city hall carrying homemade signs, demanding that their rights as homeowners be recognized. When neither the protest nor their stand at city hall produced results, a lawsuit was filed in the California Supreme Court. When the court ruled in favor of the city, the fight to save their homes was all but over. Many of those who remained refused to leave even as bulldozers leveled the homes surrounding them. The city continued to press its eminent domain but never forcibly tried to remove those who stayed. One of the reasons for the city's apparent leniency in not forcibly removing the holdouts was the rise of the "Red Scare" going on in the United States at the time. In 1952, the city's assistant director of the CHA, Frank Wilkinson, was questioned by the House Un-American Activities Committee and was subsequently fired because his Chavez Ravine housing project was judged a "socialist plot." Wilkinson would spend a year in prison over the charge. After his firing, the LA City Council tried to cancel the public housing contract the city had with the federal government, but courts ruled that the contract was legally binding. Enter Norris Paulson.

During the mayoral race of 1953, Republican Norris Paulson ran against incumbent Democrat Mayor Bowron. Paulson ran on an anti-communist platform and vowed to stop the housing project as "un-American." Using

Chavez Ravine as part of his campaign, Paulson won the election and became mayor in 1953. After his election, Paulson entered into intense negotiations with the federal government, managed to get it to drastically reduce the asking price and bought Chavez Ravine back from the feds. However, there was one stipulation: the land had to be used for public purposes. Exactly what that meant, however, was never defined, and over the intervening years several ideas, including low-cost housing, were put on the table. What finally came about as the use for Chavez Ravine stretched the idea of "public use" to almost fantastical heights.

During the 1950s, the city of Los Angeles experienced a growth spurt the likes of which had seldom been seen. Thanks to the growing car culture, folks flocking to Hollywood and the beaches and, in no small part, the spectacular weather enjoyed in Southern California, Los Angeles became a destination city for many Americans relocating after World War II. The one thing Los Angeles lacked was a major league sports team. To remedy this supposed defecit, Democrat county supervisor Kenneth Hahn, father of the well-known Janice Hahn, began looking for a team that wanted and was willing to relocate to Los Angeles. When Hahn heard that Walter O'Malley was getting frustrated with Brooklyn's reluctance to build the Dodgers a new stadium, he began courting O'Malley to move the team to Los Angeles. To O'Malley, who had already acquired the minor league Los Angeles Angels and Wrigley Field in 1957, bringing the Dodgers to LA seemed like a good fit, but even though O'Malley liked the idea, instead of playing in Wrigley Field, he wanted a new stadium built for his premier team. From the moment O'Malley made the request for a new stadium, Hahn had the perfect place in mind.

As early as 1955, Democrat Los Angeles councilwoman Rosalind Wyman had been courting O'Malley, and now that a tentative agreement had been reached, Wyman, leading the city council vote, approved the sale of Chavez Ravine—the property Kenneth Hahn thought would be perfect for the new stadium—to O'Malley to be the new home of the Los Angeles Dodgers. O'Malley had to give up Wrigley Field, but that was a small price to pay for 315 acres of land in the heart of Los Angeles. Now that the future of Chavez Ravine was set, the city once again pushed its eminent domain and began condemning the holdout homes and shops, emptying the land as quickly as possible. Several families still refused to leave the homes they had built and lived in for decades, so on May 9, 1959—a day that came to be called Black Friday by the former residents of Chavez Ravine and the Battle of Chavez Ravine by the rest of the country—Los

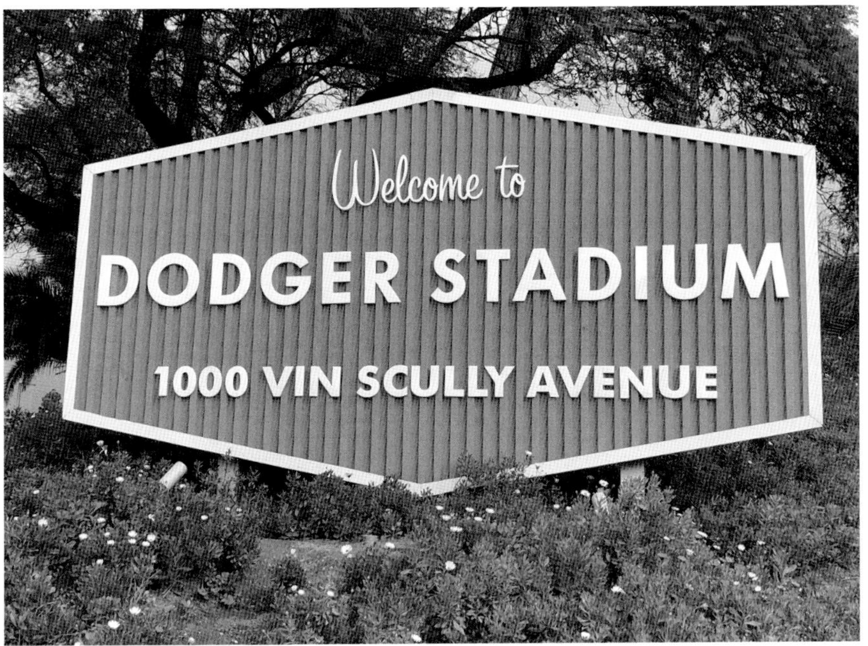

The City of Los Angeles began displacing the residents of Chavez Ravine almost two decades before they asked Walter O'Malley to move the Dodgers.

Angeles County sheriffs entered the neighborhood and began kicking in doors and forcibly removing those who refused to leave. A member of one family, the Aréchigas, was carried out of the house while sheriffs removed the family's belongings from their home, and the family was then forced to watch as a bulldozer leveled their home. Afterward, the Aréchigas set up a tent where their house once stood and lived there for a few days until they were finally forced to leave altogether.

The Dodgers moved to Los Angeles in 1958 and played in the LA Memorial Coliseum while their new stadium was being built. After the forcible removal of the residents of Chavez Ravine, construction began in earnest. Before the stadium could be built, the land had to be drastically changed and leveled. The ridge between Sulphur and Cemetery Ravines was knocked down and the ravines filled in, completely burying Palo Verde Elementary school. Groundbreaking for Dodger Stadium occurred on September 17, 1959, with the new stadium opening four years later on April 10, 1962. Even to this day, controversy about "public use" still haunts the Dodgers and Los Angeles. With all the controversy, heartache and violence involved with the forcible removal of families to make way

Dodger Stadium is now the third-oldest baseball stadium in the United States—and maybe its most haunted.

The Palo Verde Elementary School still lies buried somewhere under Dodger Stadium's parking lot.

for a sports team, it shouldn't come as a surprise that Dodger Stadium may be haunted.

Baseball is not something that most folks associate with ghosts. The game is the American pastime: it's fun, it's exciting, it's a great way for families to spend an afternoon or evening out with hot dogs, peanuts and cold drinks. Why on earth would anyone think about ghosts when thinking about baseball? As strange and unexpected as it is, many baseball stadiums are indeed haunted, and Dodger Stadium certainly falls into that category. Over the years, many reports and stories have come from Chavez Ravine of spirits hanging around the stadium and grounds. One such story may or may not be paranormal but has been told so many times that trying to explain it away as Los Angeles fog is, shall we say, troublesome at best. Folks have reported seeing a strange mist rise out of nowhere as if coming up from the ground. It is never thick enough to obscure or cause a problem with the game, but when it comes up on the field, everyone in the stadium can see it. The strangest thing about this mist is that it isn't always relegated to the field. People say that this same mist has been seen coming up all over the stadium: in the stands, near the concessions and even in the parking lots. No one has ever figured out exactly where the mist comes from or been able to predict when it might appear, but it has become common enough that season ticketholders, employees and players have become used to it.

Another spirit, according to local—or urban—legend, is that of a woman who killed her own children back before Dodger Stadium was built. It is believed that sometime in the 1920s, a mother, living in Chavez Ravine in the early days, having become despondent over what she perceived to be her abject poverty, decided that it would be better for her and her children to pass from this mortal plane of existence. Ever since that time, this "woman in white" has been seen wandering the area as if looking for something; many believe that she is looking for her children. Legend says that the murder/suicide allowed her children to pass through the veil while forcing her to remain behind, forever separated from her children. After the stadium was built, employees began seeing this lost and forlorn mother moving through the seats, hallways and tunnels of the stadium, still looking for her kids. Other employees have said they have seen this same woman in white diving over one of the cliffs near the stadium. Could this be the method she chose for her murder/suicide?

On many occasions, a couple has been seen at the top of one of the hillsides that make up what is left of Chavez Ravine. Urban legend says these were honeymooners who, while taking in the lights and sights of Los

Angeles from this hilltop one evening, somehow plummeted to their deaths. It is unclear exactly what happened; however, folks who have seen the two lovers say that the couple rises from their seat, one of them (it is never certain which one) begins to fall down the hill, the other attempts to save their partner and they both tumble down the hill to their deaths.

Perhaps the most told and the most misunderstood tales come from the fact that a cemetery once stood where Dodger Stadium's parking lot is now. It is not unusual for folks who come early to tailgate or who stay late while traffic clears to see spirits wandering around the south parking lot. It is here that the Hebrew Benevolent Society once had its cemetery. As most people know, deceased humans loath having their bodies removed from their eternal sleep, and when they are disinterred for the sake of relocation, it should not be surprising that their spirit becomes restless and possibly lost. This may be what is happening in the Dodger Stadium parking lot. The spirits that are seen here are dressed in clothes that look like they are from the early twentieth century, which would fit the description of those who were buried here in the Jewish cemetery. It is believed that the ghosts are now wandering in hopes of finding their missing bodies. No one is sure if this is the case, but hopefully, it is possible to lead these lost spirits to their new resting places so they can be at peace. It is said, mistakenly, that the cemetery was moved to make way for Dodger Stadium; however, history says that the remains and monuments of the Hebrew Benevolent Society Cemetery were moved in 1910 to the Home of Peace Cemetery in East Los Angeles, which was established by the Congregation B'nai B'rith. Murderer Dr. Harold Perelson, known for his Los Feliz Murder Mansion (which he is said to haunt) is buried at the same Home of Peace Cemetery. (For more information on this murder and its ghosts, see my book *Hollywood Obscura*.)

Real Ghost Stories Online is a podcast that delves into ghost stories from all over the world. During their March 16, 2015 show, the hosts talked about an employee at Dodger Stadium who called to tell them about a couple of strange encounters he had while working there. The caller, an LA man named Abel who had worked at the stadium for more than twenty years, said that he had never had a paranormal encounter while working there until a couple of years ago. Because of the way the stadium is designed, he had to clock in to work on the upper level and then walk down the ramps or the stairs to the lower level where his workstation was. He said he could take the elevator, but he liked the creepiness of the stairs and the spookiness of the ramp. He said that one day he was walking down after clocking in and distinctly heard a male voice close by. He said he wasn't really paying

Remnants of Chavez Ravine can still be found at Dodger Stadium, if one looks closely.

attention, but since the voice was not more than a couple feet away, he stopped to listen because he didn't clearly make out what was being said. He figured a coworker was nearby and wanted to talk. He never heard the voice again. He looked around but saw no one, checked up and down the bannisters and stairs but couldn't find a soul. He said that if someone had been there and as close to him as the voice had been, there is no way that person could have left without him hearing them leave.

Abel went to talk to a friend and coworker who regularly works nights after the games are over and asked him if he had ever had a strange encounter at the stadium. He said his friend simply smiled at him and said, "Stick around after the game and see for yourself." Abel's friend went on to tell him that he often hears people running through the areas near the concession stands and swears that he once heard something with four legs running around but has never been able to find anyone running—or any*thing*, for that matter. He told Abel that he often hears folks talking in the seats as if watching a game, but there is no one there, even though he can hear them. Abel said that he knows people have died in the stadium and has even seen a fan die from a massive heart attack right in front of him but never thought that folks would hang around after death. But now that he is aware of the spirits, he has noticed that "the fun begins two to three hours after the night games end."

Dodger Stadium is now the third-oldest baseball stadium in the country, behind Fenway Park in Boston and Wrigley Field in Chicago, but only Dodger Stadium has the dubious distinction of having killed an entire

A large number of Hispanics make up the Dodgers' fan base; they are devoted and supportive and realize that the city, not the Dodgers organization, evicted the residents of Chavez Ravine.

neighborhood, displacing hundreds of Mexican American families. Where the stadium sits today is still called Chavez Ravine, but it is a far cry from the once-proud community that was built with hard work and love. As Democrat Los Angeles city councilman Edward Roybal, the only city official to come out in support of the residents of Chavez Ravine, said, "It is not morally or legally right for a governmental agency to condemn private land, take it away from property owners through eminent domain proceedings, then turn around and give it to a private person or corporation for private gain."

It is still unclear how land that was to remain in the public trust could be passed on to a sports magnate and why the city, courts and community did not stop the theft of the land from its rightful owners. Greed, money and a need for professional sports set a dangerous precedent that, hopefully, will never again rear its ugly head. The Dodgers are lucky. The Mexican American community's relationship was strained to the breaking point with what seemed, at the time, to be simple racism, but over the years, especially as the Dodgers became one of the winningest teams in baseball, things changed: now the team's fan base is widely Hispanic. I guess some wrongs can be forgiven with enough time.

CHAPTER 10

GRIFFITH PARK, THE TRUE HEART OF LOS ANGELES

Yes, many would dispute the idea that Griffith Park is the true heart of Los Angeles. Many would say that distinction belongs to Olvera Street, and they may be correct, as this was the birthplace of Los Angeles. Others might claim Pershing Square, the Garment District or even the entire downtown Los Angeles area are the heart of the city, but many, including this author, believe the heart of Los Angeles lies within the largest urban park in the country, Griffith Park. The reason so many folks think this has to do with the sheer number of famous LA landmarks that lie within the park itself. Griffith Observatory, the world-famous Los Angeles zoo, the Greek Theatre and the iconic Hollywood sign all sit inside Griffith Park's public lands, along with many other locations known locally and worldwide. With urban hiking trails, art museums and picturesque lakes, what other location within the City of Angels could claim to have more of a right to be called the heart of the city than Griffith Park?

As the park is now over 125 years old, many have forgotten that it was once privately owned. The history of Griffith Park is anything but a storybook tale, and there are so many twists and turns to the story that I cannot fit it all into one small chapter. The history of Griffith Park begins with Spanish explorer Juan Bautista de Anza as he led a group of colonists and soldiers from Mexico to what is today San Francisco. On that journey, the group spent the night at what today is the John Ferraro Athletic Fields (according to the 1996 book *Griffith Park: A Centennial History* by author Mike Eberts). One of the soldiers on this trip was Jose Vincent Feliz, and he fell

As well known as Griffith Park may be, most know it for its Art Deco observatory and not for its hauntings.

in love with the beauty of the area. Feliz would eventually settle in the burgeoning town of El Pueblo de Nuestra Señora la Reina de Los Angeles and be given a six-thousand-acre land grant by the Spanish government for his service to the crown. This land grant would become the Rancho Los Feliz. The town passed to Feliz's daughter-in-law Maria Verdugo, who owned the land until her death in 1861, at which time the rancho was passed on to her son, Antonio Feliz. This is where the story becomes a bit more interesting—and twisted.

The story of Griffith Park takes a wild turn when Don Antonio Feliz dies of smallpox in 1863. It is said that when Antonio's niece, Doña Petronilla, found out that her uncle left her with nothing in his will, she cursed the entire area. The story goes that not long before Don Feliz passed, Don Antonio Coronel, his longtime friend and the former mayor of Los Angeles, showed up at Rancho Los Feliz with his lawyer, Don Innocante. Moments before Feliz passed into the great beyond, he signed a new will and testament that had already been drawn up by Coronel and Innocante; to make everything look legal, members of one of the families who were ranch hands signed as witnesses and the deal was done. The will gave Feliz's sister, Soledad, who lived at Rancho Los Feliz, and his godson Juan Sanchez half the furniture, to be divided equally between them, with the second half going to Antonio's other sister, from whom many say he had become estranged. Sanchez received twelve mares, a pinto stallion and a colt from each mare. Petronilla received a grand total of nothing. All the land was bequeathed to Coronel.

If the story is to be believed, it most assuredly brings up questions about the distribution of Feliz's wealth and the timing of the new will—whose ink, it is said, was still wet as Don Antonio died. Suffice it to say, if the story is true, the Feliz family, and especially Petronilla, would have had the absolute right to be very upset. Petronilla, in fact, may have been so angry that she set a curse not only on the Coronel and Innocante families but also on the land itself. After Don Feliz's death, the will was contested, and Innocante testified that Feliz had been rendered speechless just hours before the will was rewritten and could only move his head as Innocante and Coronel wrote the will, approving each section with a nod. The will was upheld in court, to which Petronilla, speaking directly to the judge, Coronel and Innocante, said,

> *The one shall die an untimely death, the other in blood and violence. A blight shall fall upon the face of this terrestrial paradise. The cattle shall no longer fatten but sicken on its own pastures, the fields shall no longer respond to the toil of the tiller. The grand oaks shall wither and die. The wrath of heaven and vengeance of hell shall fall upon this place….No man shall ever enjoy a profit from the rancho and misfortune, rime and death will follow.*

Many folks strongly believe in the curse, some are undecided and even more believe that the curse is nothing more than a hoax and will actually disparage those who entertain the thought of its validity. I, as always, will leave you, the reader, to decide what you want to believe—but that being said, since the curse became known, many odd and unusual things have gone on within this urban paradise.

For starters, the lawyer who drew up the new will and testament that Don Feliz signed was shot and killed in a bar fight not long after Petronilla's curse stated that one would die in violence and bloodshed. The judge died less than a year after his decision to uphold the obviously tainted document, and although Coronel lived until the 1870s, he was plagued with various illnesses, beginning shortly after the curse was made, and watched as those close to him suffered their own losses and sicknesses. When Coronel finally passed, his wife inherited the rancho, but things were already on the decline.

The Hollywood sign and surrounding hills (here, as seen from Griffith Observatory) have all shown, by the many tales that come from the area, that ghosts roam the park and the curse of Griffith Park may exist.

Coronel's widow remarried; however, her new husband's demeanor was more than she could take, and bitter divorce proceedings ensued, which wiped out any fortune she had left.

Charles V. Howard bought the rancho, and he was later shot dead in a local saloon, and the next owner was killed by bandits in a bloody shoot-out. Leon "Lucky" Baldwin then purchased the rancho, and his nickname was no help in warding off the curse Petronilla laid on the land. Baldwin had dreams of building the rancho into a thriving farm and cattle ranch, but after a plague of grasshoppers destroyed the fields, with the cattle starving and diseases spreading through the herd, Baldwin was forced to mortgage the ranch. Lucky had already spent a small fortune building a new home for his brother, John, and after a brushfire spread through the rancho, destroying the rest of his assets, Lucky was forced to sell. John Baldwin, Lucky's brother, was later killed by Mexican bandits.

Thomas Bell purchased the Rancho Los Feliz from Baldwin, and his fate is shrouded in mystery. It is said that Bell either tripped and fell from the top of the stairway in his mansion, killing him, or that an angry mistress pushed him as they were descending the staircase, hoping he would break his neck. Whichever story one wishes to believe, Thomas Bell was, in fact, killed falling down the stairs in his home.

In December 1882, Griffith J. Griffith purchased 4,071 acres of the Rancho Los Feliz (the rest of the acreage had been sold off in prior years). Griffith was born in Wales and immigrated to the United States. He was not a man of means on arriving in his new country but was determined to live the American dream and had more than succeeded by the time he became the rancho's owner. Griffith lived in peace on the rancho for two years until a particularly violent electrical storm hit in 1884. This storm was just the beginning of the troubles the curse had in store for Griffith and may be the reason he was the last private owner of what would become Griffith Park.

There is a story that says a severe electrical storm hit Rancho Los Feliz in 1884, but I have not been able to find evidence of this occurring in the National Weather database. This does not mean the event never happened, just that it may have been too localized to be noted. Regardless, the story says that the wind, rain and thunderous lightning caused "the best part of the ranch to be swept away to the sea." Rancho Los Feliz is more than forty miles away from the coast, but many believe that the torrent sent a mudslide down its many streams into the Los Angeles River and then to the river's terminus at Long Beach Harbor. Whatever the case may be, according to a local news report at the time, a violent storm swept across the LA basin,

Ostrich Farm, Los Angeles. *From the New York Public Library.*

stripping away the vegetation from the rancho and killing much of the livestock. Several people claimed that during the storm, they saw the ghost of Dona Petronilla drifting about, renewing her curse. Another report stated that the ghost of Don Antonio Feliz was seen along with demons who were plainly riding waves and directing torrents onto the land. Baron Griffith escaped to town at midnight.

As far-fetched as these reports may seem, Griffith himself appeared to believe the tales. It is said that after this night, Griffith would never set foot on his own property unless it was during daylight hours and would retreat to his home at the first sign of twilight. After the storm and the reports that followed, ghost stories about Rancho Los Feliz were the talk of the town. The citizens of Los Angeles were coming to know this rancho as the most haunted place in the area. It would also seem that the storm reignited the curse.

The year following the devastating storm, Griffith partnered with naturalist Charles Sketchley, who moved his ostrich amusement park from Orange County to the rancho, where 680 acres were set aside and the public was invited to come and view the big birds. Griffith and Sketchley built a railway that took folks to see the birds; visitors could also buy ostrich feathers to take home as souvenirs. Even though the bird farm seemed to be a hit with the public, the ghost stories and the fact that that the farm was closed promptly before dark made many reluctant to pay more than once to visit the attraction. The ostrich farm and partnership with Sketchley ended only four years later, in 1889, with both men losing quite a bit of money in the process.

Two years after the bird farm shut down, Frank Burkett, a former employee of the bird farm and tenant who rented a small cottage on the farm, attempted to kill Griffith with a double-barreled shotgun. Having been evicted from the grounds after the farm shuttered and he failed to pay his rent, Burkett blamed Griffith, who had filed a lawsuit against him over the matter, for his ruination. Burkett, luckily for Griffith, knew little about shotguns and loaded the gun with birdshot rather than the buckshot he had intended to use. This saved Griffith from death, but Burkett then committed suicide with a revolver, thinking he had killed his intended target. The curse seemed to have claimed another victim.

In 1887, Griffith met Christina Mesmer, the daughter of a wealthy hotelier. The Mesmer family were descendants of the Verdugo family, whose kin once owned the rancho. This could be why Griffith and Christina were introduced by Christina's father in the first place—although Christina was heir to a vast fortune, and the family tried to make sure Griffith never claimed that inheritance. They were married later that year, but after their nuptials, "Tina" Griffith began to think she may have made a mistake. Griffith J. Griffith was widely known as a pompous man, even calling himself "Colonel" Griffith even though there was and is nothing to confirm this title. One account stated that Griffith was "only a roly-poly pompous little fellow with an exaggerated strut like a turkey gobbler and a midget egomaniac braggart." However, by all outward appearances, their marriage looked like a good union, even though there were many contentious moments occurring behind the scenes. It all came to head in 1903, while Griffith and his wife Tina vacationed in Santa Monica, California.

The couple and their teenage son, Vandell, were enjoying the amenities in the Presidential Suite at the Arcadia Hotel when, on September 3, 1903, Griffith became paranoid that there might be something going on with his wife behind his back; he seemed to believe that Tina, a Catholic, and the Pope were conspiring to poison him due to his Protestant religion. Griffith forced his wife to her knees, asked her questions at gunpoint and then pulled

Travel Town and its haunted train cars also lie within Griffith Park.

the trigger. Tina turned her head away at the precise moment the gun was fired, but the bullet struck the side of her face; she then leapt for the window and jumped out of the room. Luckily for Tina Griffith, the Presidential Suite was directly over another roof, which broke her fall enough to save her life. Tina was taken to a hospital by hotel staff; Griffith was taken to jail by the Santa Monica police.

During Griffith's trial for attempted murder, both his son and his wife testified against him. When Tina Griffith took the stand, she unveiled her face, showing the jury her permanently disfigurement and her missing eye. The jury returned a unanimous verdict of guilty as charged. Despite the verdict, it would seem that Griffith's reputation preceded him. Having donated 3,015 acres of land to Los Angeles in 1896, Griffith had cemented his standing with many in LA, and this was most likely the reason for his light sentence of only two years in San Quentin Prison; of that sentence, he would only serve twenty months. Tina was granted a divorce after the trial and was given full custody of their son, Vandell, and cash from the Griffith estate. Griffith, on his release, was said to be a changed man, but many still believe that to have been just another of his acts. Urban legend has it that this story is simply another chapter in the life of the curse and more proof of its existence.

After his release, Griffith became interested in prison reform and deeply involved with the development of what was now Griffith Park. When Griffith donated the land to Los Angeles on December 16, 1896, many believed he did it strictly as a tax write-off for his failed and costly attempt at farming. He told the city,

> *Recognizing the duty which one who has acquired some little wealth owes to the community in which he prospered and desiring to aid the advancement and happiness of the city that has for so long, and always will be my home, I am impelled to make an offer, the acceptance of which by yourselves, acting for the people, I believe will be a source of enjoyment and pride to my fellows and add charm to our beloved city.…I hereby propose to present to Los Angeles, as a Christmas gift, a public park of about three thousand acres.*

No one can deny the generosity of the gift, but knowing that Griffith was a selfish man, many wonder about the timing of the donation. Knowing that he had just married into an extremely wealthy family, along with a disastrous showing in running Rancho Los Feliz and his supposed belief in the curse and ghosts haunting the land, it is not hard to believe he was just trying to unload property he longer desired. Griffith also set some rules according to which the land would be donated: it would be kept as a place of refuge, rest and recreation for the masses; rail fares would be capped at a nickel so that the park could be accessed by all, regardless of income level; and it had to be called Griffith Park, forever.

Griffith had once visited the Mount Wilson Observatory and, since that time, had wanted to build an observatory where common folk could look at the heavens. So in 1912, Griffith attempted to give Los Angeles money to build the Griffith Observatory, but the city flatly turned down the offer. Griffith had fallen out of favor with the folks of Los Angeles after his conviction, and Mount Griffith, where the observatory was to be built, had already had its name changed to Mount Hollywood. However, after Griffith passed away in July 1919, the city, having been named the recipient of the money for the observatory's construction in Griffith's will, relented rather than fight through the legal hurdles of refusing the cash, and the spectacular Art Deco Griffith Observatory opened in May 1935. Not only was the $1 million donation earmarked for the observatory, but Griffith had also instructed the city to build an outdoor theater with Greek aesthetics and columns. The cornerstone of what would become

A children's ride couldn't escape the curse: a woman's body was found hanging from a tree and on fire near this carousel. Her ghost is said to still haunt the ride, which is now permanently closed.

the famous Greek Theatre was laid in 1928, and the first production was presented there on June 26, 1931.

Griffith Park is now a place where families can come to see the world-famous zoo or a spectacular stage production as good as any Broadway show, hike and ride horses through a plethora of urban wilderness trails or even venture through historic railcars that harken back to a past all but forgotten. There was even an old historic carousel folks could ride to bring back the feeling of a peaceful country fair. With all the nostalgia and family fun going on, one might ask, "What happened to the curse?" Unfortunately, the curse still seems to be with us and the land itself.

Over the years since Griffith Park became a public oasis in the middle of Los Angeles, many things have happened here that defy logic in their frequency. The park has become a literal dumping ground for human bodies; granted, its remote trails and thick brush are a determining factor, yet the sheer number of murder victims found is astronomical. During the Hillside Stranglers' reign of terror, Griffith Park was their go-to dumping ground, and that trend has continued to this day. A blanket-wrapped body was found just off a hiking trail, bodies are frequently found in the park's bathrooms and transmission towers, a coroner's dog retrieved a severed head and other

The Astronomers Monument at Griffith Observatory, 2013. *Highsmith, Carol M, photographer, via Library of Congress.*

body parts of victims believed to have been disposed of in the park and a burning body was even found hanging from a tree limb in broad daylight; authorities ruled the death a suicide. Hopefully this trend will not continue, but it seems the curse is still alive and well.

As for the lost souls who call the land home, they, too, are still present. In 1923, the now-famous Hollywood sign, then the Hollywoodland sign, was erected, and only nine years later, Peg Entwistle flung herself from the *H*, killing herself; Peg still haunts the sign to this day. Doña Petronilla is still seen on occasion, perhaps checking on her curse; Don Antonio is glimpsed near his old homestead as well as Bee Rock, now the site of the old Los Angeles Zoo; and Don Coronel is still hanging around, if the reports are true. Lovers are said to haunt picnic table no. 29, although this may be more urban legend than fact. From phantom hikers to ghostly lovers, murder victims and even zoo animals, Griffith Park is said to be one of the most—if not *the* most—haunted places in Los Angeles.

Whatever one thinks about Griffith J. Griffith, he helped create one of the most spectacular parks in the world and left his name not only throughout the park but throughout the world as well. The park has a place in the history not only of the area but also of the world that is hard to deny. It was here that Walt Disney had the idea to create Disneyland while watching his children play. It was here that the first "gay-in" was held on Memorial Day 1968, to help free homosexuals from the torments of bigotry. It was here that Babe Ruth learned that he had been traded from the Red Sox to the Yankees and where 750 Quonset huts were set up to house returning World War II veterans after the war ended. It is even the place where a lone mountain lion became the unofficial yet unapproachable mascot and pet of an entire city. Haunted, cursed yet magical and loved by all, Griffith Park is truly the haunted heart of Los Angeles.

CHAPTER 11

THE SAD SPIRIT OF THE HOLLYWOOD SIGN

The Hollywood sign is known worldwide and has become a symbol for millions of folks around the world as the gateway to Tinseltown and dreams of stardom, wealth and fame. This sign, as famous as it is, is still mostly a mystery to those who know and revere it and the city for which it stands. Most don't even realize it isn't technically even in Hollywood—the Hollywood Hills, yes; the city of Hollywood, no. The arguably most famous sign in the world is actually in the city of Los Angeles, within the boundaries of Griffith Park—situated near the top of Mount Lee (formerly Mount Griffith). Few know about the history of the sign: how it was meant to stand for only eighteen months, that it was all but destroyed numerous times over the years and how it has had a dark history from the moment it was erected. There is certainly more to this iconic grouping of letters than most people know—or want to know.

The city of Hollywood grew in prominence around the year 1912, and after Carl Laemmle opened Universal City in 1915, there was no stopping the film industry. Moviemaking studios began popping up all over Hollywood. As Americans became more and more interested in films and in becoming the next big star, folks began to flock to Hollywood in ever increasing numbers. Many of these folks were affluent, and many were looking for homes to reflect their social standing. So in the early 1920s, a group of entrepreneurs headed by railroad tycoon Eli P. Clark, along with real estate developers Moses Sherman, Tracy Shoults and Sidney Woodruff, teamed up with *Los Angeles Times* publisher Harry Chandler

The Hollywood sign can be seen from over twenty miles away on a clear day, from all around Los Angeles.

to build an exclusive community called Hollywoodland on the hillside overlooking Hollywood.

There is some speculation about why the suffix *-land* was added to the name, but common lore says that it was part of a marketing ploy to capitalize on Lewis Carroll's *Alice's Adventures in Wonderland* or J.M. Barrie's Neverland from his book *Peter Pan*, or perhaps both. Whatever the reason might have been, Hollywoodland became the new development's name. The reasoning behind the name itself may be mildly disputed, but the idea behind the new billboard will most likely always be arguable. Therefore, I will not get into the weeds of the actual origins of the Hollywoodland billboard; I'll only say that it may have been the most brilliant advertising ploy ever created. I say this due to the fact that the Hollywood sign was nothing more than an advertisement for the Hollywoodland housing project and was never meant to stand for more than a year and a half while the homes were being sold.

Even though the Hollywood sign began life simply as a billboard, for an advertisement, its cost was astronomical at the time. The total cost of the sign was a whopping $21,000, or approximately $370,000 in today's money, a tidy sum indeed. When completed, each letter of the Hollywoodland billboard stood thirty feet wide and forty-five feet tall, and just over four thousand lights covered the entire sign so that it could be seen throughout the Los Angeles basin in three directions from miles away as night fell on Griffith Park. It took almost a year to erect, and when the sign was first lit, during a grand unveiling celebration, the *Los Angeles Evening Express* reported, "The gigantic electric sign, the largest in the world, vies with the stars in the luminous beauty." On that day, unbeknownst to the world, a legend was born.

After the masses witnessed the sign light up in spectacular fashion, the *Los Angeles Times* began running regular advertisements telling perspective buyers how Hollywoodland was a "refuge from city living." The Hollywoodland sign not only advertised the new housing development, but by the mid-1920s, it had also come to symbolize the city and all it had to offer. As such, the sign was granted regular maintenance, remaining a bright pictogram for Hollywood, its studios and its exciting nightlife. The sign had become an icon almost overnight, inspiring the hopes and dreams of folks all over the country. Unfortunately, it wasn't meant to last. When the Great Depression hit, home sales declined along with the tourist trade. Even though Hollywood, with its ongoing movie productions and star power, was never hit as hard by the economic downturn as other places, money was still tight, and in 1933, the decision was made to end all the maintenance the Hollywoodland sign had enjoyed up to that point.

Without a dedicated maintenance budget, it didn't take long for the elements to begin affecting the sign. On September 19, 1936, the second *O* collapsed during a severe windstorm, and after an inspection of the sign, a letter was sent stating that the sign was "too badly dried, split and warped and no money should be spent fiddling around with the sign." In the next three years, two more letters of the sign would collapse and were simply allowed to stay where they fell. Then, in early 1944, strong winds once again hit Griffith Park, causing the opening letter *H* to come crashing down. This was enough for the M.H. Sherman Company, which, in December that same year, donated what was left of the Hollywoodland sign and the surrounding 425-acre site to the City of Los Angeles. The city formally accepted the offer in January 1945, making the iconic Hollywoodland sign the property of the citizens of Los Angeles.

Los Angeles incorporated the sign and acreage into the boundaries of Griffith Park and placed it under the jurisdiction of the parks commission. The commission was unsure what to do with the sign, so it did nothing. Debate continued within city chambers, and in 1947, with the Los Angeles Parks and Rec Commission calling the now-dilapidated sign an "eyesore," the decision was made to tear the whole thing down. What the city hadn't taken into account was how Hollywood had come to feel about "their" sign. With protests springing up all over Hollywood, and the residents of Hollywoodland taking part, the City of Los Angeles began to waver about destroying the sign. That's when the Hollywood Chamber of Commerce stepped in, offering the city a choice. The chamber would refurbish the sign and replace the missing letters, but only if it could remove the last four letters of the famous sign. The chamber wanted it to simply read, "Hollywood." It took two years of negotiations between the city and the chamber, but in April 1949, the city gave the chamber of commerce permission to restore the sign. Thus the famous and iconic Hollywoodland sign, with all the history surrounding its creation, became simply the Hollywood sign.

The next decade saw another marked decline in the upkeep and care of the iconic sign. There had been half-hearted attempts to keep the sign standing, and a caretaker had been assigned; however, not much was done to keep the Hollywood sign from decaying in the elements. As the 1960s dawned, Hollywood residents began to move out of the clustered city, headed for the suburban San Fernando Valley. Not only were the citizens leaving the crowded metropolis, but the studios were leaving as well. By 1970, only Paramount Studios remained in Hollywood—along with the smaller, lesser-known studios that had sprouted up over the years. The City of Hollywood was in decline, while the porn industry was on the rise. Many of the major theaters began showing skin flicks, and smaller venues followed suit. Adult bookstores and theaters, massage parlors and seedy bars became the main staple of Hollywood. As tourism dwindled due to drugs and crime, the infrastructure of the city was in full decline, and Hollywood was no longer seen as Tinseltown but more as a drug mecca. As the city's tax base shrank, so did the importance of keeping the Hollywood sign pristine for the tourists who were no longer coming to town. The early 1970s saw the sign standing as a rusted and sad symbol of a city in the same state of decay.

As the sign began to literally crumble under its own weight, the Los Angeles Cultural Heritage Board stepped in, designating the sign Cultural Monument No. 111. With this new recognition, the Hollywood Chamber of Commerce stepped back in to form two committees to help raise funds for and awareness about the sign in hopes of once again restoring the newly minted monument. Many fundraisers were held with money rolling in for restoration, and on September 14, 1973, a celebration was held for the partially restored sign. Silent film star Gloria Swanson had the honor of throwing the switch for the temporary floodlights that illuminated the sign for the entire area to see. As it happened, a thick fog rolled in just as the lights came on, obscuring the sign for everyone except those in attendance. This fog may have foreshadowed things to come, as on February 10, 1978, a strong wind damaged every letter of the sign, with the third *O* suffering broken and twisted beams, snapped guide wires and broken poles. The *Y* partially collapsed, and panels of sheet metal were blown off every other letter and taken away by the wind. It was later revealed that the simple facelift the chamber of commerce gave the iconic sign was woefully inadequate.

Once again, the chamber held fundraisers for the sign, and this time stars such as Hugh Hefner, Groucho Marx and rocker Alice Cooper, as well as Warner Bros. Studios, stepped in with large donations to help the historic monument. The old Hollywood sign was completely demolished and hauled away, and the hillside was empty and barren for the first time in fifty-five years. Immediately after removal of the old sign, work began on a new, more sturdy icon using modern techniques and material meant to have the new Hollywood sign standing for many, many years. On November 11, 1978, the Hollywood Chamber of Commerce held a gala at the Griffith Park Observatory (one of the best places to see the sign) for the grand unveiling of the Hollywood sign we see today.

As historic as the Hollywood(land) sign might be, there is a darker side to this icon that many folks know and others have yet to touch on. Ghosts,

The open-air Greek Theatre in Griffith Park is very near the Hollywood sign. It is said that the spirits of the sign also haunt the Greek.

curses and urban legends surround the iconic sign on the side of Mount Lee. Being in Griffith Park, Mount Lee (once Mount Griffith) couldn't escape the curse Doña Petronilla placed on the entire area. Many believe the curse is the main reason that so much has gone wrong with the Hollywood sign over the years: the corrosion and decay, always followed by freakish and destructive winds and thunderstorms that tear down large sections of the sign itself. There is also an urban legend tied to the same curse that says a strange cryptid prowls around the sign. It is sometimes said to be a chupacabra and at other times described as a large bearlike creature with glowing red eyes and snarling, drooling teeth. These stories are few and far between and may simply be tales to frighten children or told around a campfire. Then there are the ghost stories.

According to one story that has sprung up in recent years, the ghost of Eden Ahbez has been seen at the foot of the first *L* of the sign since his death in 1995. Ahbez, born George Alexander Aberle, came to Los Angeles in the mid-1940s and joined up with a group of "nature mystics" that changed his life. Ahbez is best known for his songwriting ability and his composition that led to one of Nat King Cole's biggest hits, "Nature Boy." Ahbez never cared about money, fame or possessions and often lived off the land or the goodwill of others, and one of his favorite spots to live was at the foot of one *L* in the Hollywood sign. It was his love of this area that many believe brings Eden Ahbez back here in his afterlife.

Another spirit that may haunt the Hollywood sign is that of former caretaker Albert Kothe. Kothe, a German immigrant, was first employed as a handyman/caretaker by the Hollywoodland real estate company. His job was mainly to change lightbulbs and make minor repairs. This may sound like a simple task, but with 3,700 lightbulbs in the sign, it was anything but an easy job. Lights would routinely burn out, at which point Albert would inevitably need to grab a ladder and a new bulb from the shack that sat behind the sign, scurry up and unscrew the bulb, install the new one, return all his tools of the trade to the shack—only to find another bulb had burned out and he would have to repeat the process once more. It has been said that Albert Kothe lived in the shack where all the things he needed were stored. The truth of the matter was that he lived nearby on North Beachwood Drive, as the shack had no plumbing and what was needed for the upkeep of the sign barely fit inside; it would not have been possible to live in those conditions. Regardless of where Kothe actually lived, one thing is certain: he took his job seriously and seemed to enjoy the work.

The shack behind the sign is now gone and the 3,700 bulbs just a memory, but it has been said that Albert Kothe has remained and still performs this job in death that he had in life. Folks have reported seeing a wispy figure moving behind the Hollywood sign in what they say is a "purposeful way," as if it is busy doing work. On other occasions, it is said, this same figure can be seen as if climbing a ladder, fiddling about on one of the letters and descending, only to disappear as his feet touch the ground. The sign had four of its lighted letters removed by the Hollywood Chamber of Commerce, but that was after Kothe had already moved on to another job; folks who have seen him up on his ladder say that the oddest thing is when he is working on one of the now-missing letters. He may not be the most famous handyman, but he was well-known enough, at least in Hollywood, that a short movie was produced featuring Dick Van Dyke as Albert Kothe.

As compelling as the spirits of Eden Ahbez and Albert Kothe may be, they are relatively unknown and overshadowed by the sad spirit of Peg Entwistle. Peg Entwistle was born in 1908 in Wales, Great Britain; her given name was Lillian Millicent Entwistle. After her parents divorced, Peg moved to New York with her father, who became a stagehand, so while growing up, Peg always dreamed of performing onstage. Her father remarried, but both he and Peg's stepmother passed away, so she and her half brothers went to live with their aunt and uncle in Ohio. Even with this unexpected move to the Midwest, Peg never gave up her dream of making it as an actress. When Peg turned seventeen, she began pursuing a career onstage, and by 1925, she had appeared in several Broadway shows. It is rumored that a young Bette Davis, after seeing Entwistle perform, stated that she wanted to be just like her on stage.

In 1927, Peg Entwistle married fellow actor Robert Keith, who, unbeknownst to Peg, had been married once before and had a son, future actor Brian Keith. Once Entwistle found this out, her marriage fell apart, and she divorced Keith shortly thereafter, in 1929. Peg still received roles on Broadway, but once the Great Depression hit, shows became few and far between, so she decided to head to the West Coast to pursue a career in Hollywood. Once in Los Angeles, Peg moved into her uncle Charles's home and began looking for roles. So many other women were flocking to Hollywood for the same reason that Peg was getting lost in the throng of beautiful women and struggled to stand out or to get film roles. She did get a few smaller parts in studio movies, but the roles were not what she expected.

Peg's talent didn't go unnoticed, and in 1932, she finally received her first big role in a movie titled *Thirteen Women*. Peg had just finished the film when she discovered that most of her performance had been left on the cutting room floor and she had been released from her contract with RKO Pictures. With no money, no contract and no means of supporting herself, Peg sank into a deep depression. It had been hard enough to distinguish herself once, and she wasn't really looking forward to having to prove herself once again. So on the night of September 16, 1932, Peg Entwistle hiked up the canyon of Mount Lee, found the caretaker's ladder, climbed to the top of the Hollywoodland sign's *H* and threw herself to the ground below. She was killed instantly.

The following morning, a female hiker discovered a shoe directly below the sign. A bit farther down, she found a jacket and a purse, and looking farther down the mountain, the hiker saw the body of a woman and called authorities. Inside the purse, the police found a note that read, "I am afraid, I am a coward. I am sorry for everything. If I had done this a long time ago, it would have saved a lot of pain. P.E." Peg Entwistle's death was ruled a suicide, and the newspapers had a field day. The story became a national news event, and this, mixed in with Peg's minor stardom and the conspiracies and conjecture that always seem to spring up around Hollywood, helped make Peg Entwistle a legend even before her burial. One of the urban legends about Peg sprang up two months later when her film *Thirteen Women* was released. Although most of Peg's performance had been cut from the movie, what remained was a scene in which her character was to commit suicide because a "Swami" had given her and twelve of her sorority sisters prophecies of doom, causing them to take their own lives. The film, dealing with suicide, lesbianism and other subjects that were taboo at this time in the United States, was not well received.

Peg Entwistle may, in the past, have become a legend because of her suicide, but today Peg is more known for never leaving the mortal plane after her death. Many folks have heard about the "Ghost of the Hollywood Sign." Over the years, witnesses have come forth with stories of seeing Peg around the sign where she ended her life. One of the first stories came about in the 1940s, just after the *H* of the sign suddenly fell over. Folks began speculating that it was Entwistle who had caused it to topple, and many others claimed to have seen her around the fallen letter. Park rangers have claimed to see a pretty blonde woman in 1930s attire wandering the trails of Griffith Park. They say that she seems to wander aimlessly and always wears a sad look on her face and smells of gardenias, Peg's favorite perfume. They say that when they try to approach this woman to see if she is in need of help, the specter vanishes from sight. These reports have been coming in almost since the time of her death.

This same story of a seemingly lost and disoriented blonde woman has been told so many times that it is hard to ignore. It is possible that the urban legend has become so ingrained in people's psyches that they now simply evoke the sad spirit of Peg when roaming Griffith Park, but that doesn't account for the many foreign tourists who also report this phenomenon. One such report comes from a French couple honeymooning in Hollywood who said that they tried to help an obviously distraught woman who simply vanished before their eyes. They said the woman was blonde and wearing "old-style" clothing, and they had never heard of Peg Entwisle—at least that's what they told rangers when explaining what had happened.

There are stories from the 1990s about a couple who supposedly had never heard of Entwisle seeing a "disoriented blonde woman dressed in 1930s clothing" vanishing before their eyes and Brentwood Canyon residents out walking their dogs seeing Peg wandering around the neighborhood, "sad and lonely," before vanishing from sight, along with a more recent report from the Syfy Channel's show *Paranormal Witness*: four friends decided to ignore the off-limits sign and were heading up and over the fence when one of them slipped and fell down the hill, only to see a figure walking toward him, whom he said was "a woman, wearing a dress similar to the style of

Peg Entwistle may have thrown herself off the *H*, but she is not the only one to haunt the Hollywood sign.

the 1930s." He went on to say, "She wore heels and a veil over her head and face. She walked effortlessly up the hill; her footsteps made no sound." The four friends stated that it wasn't until later that they heard about the death of Peg Entwistle. Although this is the only time Peg has reportedly been seen with a veil over her face, who are we to say it couldn't have been her?

The Hollywood sign has achieved celebrity status and pop culture fame. Tourists flock to see the now-famous sign, which has appeared in many movies, TV shows and music videos. In 1998, the sign was depicted with angels standing atop its letters in the cult classic film *City of Angels*, and in the 2009 young adult film *Percy Jackson & the Olympians: The Lightning Thief*, the *H* of the sign was the gate to Hades. The sign has also made numerous appearances in "reality" TV shows that specialize in paranormal subjects and has been destroyed in so many disaster movies that I could fill a chapter on that alone. Even with all the fame the Hollywood(land) sign enjoys, we mustn't forget that its true place in history falls within the boundaries of the largest urban park in the world, Griffith Park, or that the sign itself has also had its toll of human suffering, mixed with times of joy and sadness—the entire range of human emotions. It may simply be an inert sign welcoming folks to Hollywood, but in its own way, it has always had a life—and afterlife—of its own.

CHAPTER 12

GHOSTS OF THE OLD LOS ANGELES (GRIFFITH PARK) ZOO

Everybody loves the zoo: watching the apes play and tumble around with each other, seeing how the elephants respect their family units, watching as the chimpanzees mimic the funny-looking humans who stand and gawk at them from behind their fencing. From zebras, gnu and gazelle to lions and tigers and bears, oh my—how we all love to watch the exotic and unusual animals of our world. As much as we love our time at the zoo, not many folks think about what it takes to keep the animals alive and well, all the details that go into not only the care of the animals but also what it takes to make their lives comfortable and their minds, at the very least, content. With all the work that is needed to keep animals safe, it is surprisingly easy to get it wrong. When this happens, animals become miserable and fall sick and many die; this is a form of torture for these creatures and one they don't deserve. Most folks don't think about what happens when these animals die, but the old Los Angeles Zoo at Griffith Park may hold clues about whether or not animals can come back as ghosts and spirits.

In 1907, the *Los Angeles Times* wrote, "Griffith Park is an ideal location for a zoological garden." Even though there were already a couple of zoos in Los Angeles (namely the Eastlake Zoo and the Selig Zoo), many believed that Griffith Park—in keeping with its founder's belief that the park should be a "place of recreation and rest for the masses"—was perfect for a new and improved zoo. The zoo would not become a reality until 1912, and even though support among citizens was strong, that wasn't to be the case with investors or the city council. The zoo was placed on the same grounds as a failed ostrich farm endeavor, which helped save on costs for new enclosures (a few animals that had also been attractions at the farm were left behind when it closed), and parking and guest facilities were already mostly in place, including a rundown tourist railway.

When the Griffith Park Zoo opened, its animal population was meager, with only those animals that had been left behind when the ostrich farm closed and those that had been "loaned out" by railroad tycoon Frank Murphy's private zoo. However, by 1913, the scandal-ridden Eastlake Park Zoo had sent more than one hundred frail and sick animals after authorities shut the place down for animal abuse and cruelty. Unfortunately, the Griffith Park Zoo had opened while still incomplete and now had even more animals to care for, adding to the veterinary costs. Griffith Park historian Mike Eberts wrote:

> *At first many of the animals were put into stockades: welded wire encircling groups of trees. Various livestock, wolves, monkeys and even some big cats were enclosed this way. The bear had a more natural home: they lived in the caves on a steep hillside. In 1914, an aviary, bear pits and assorted cages were built by 1,200 unemployed men....In 1916, the park commission allocated $1,500 to build suitable paddocks for deer, elk, antelope and buffalo.*

As you can see, things didn't start out rosy for the new zoo in Los Angeles. It also didn't help that the Griffith Park Zoo had to compete with the touring Bostock Collection of animals, the Barnes Wild Animal Circus and the much larger Selig Zoo, now in Lincoln Park.

Over the years, the Griffith Park Zoo did see many folks pass through its gates to see the growing collection of animals, many donated by fly-by-night animal shows and family-run zoos that had failed. But even though guests came, the zoo's reputation was sinking fast, especially within the city that at first bragged about its "world-class" zoo. Wolves, monkeys, deer and exotic cats were housed in small, unfit cages; the bears lived in tiny caves on the hillside and jerry-rigged enclosures that many animals began to escape from. It is lucky that the zoo did not host a hippopotamus at this time, and even though I hate hippothetical questions, I shudder to think what would have happened if one had escaped. To make matters worse, in 1916, sewage was found to be draining into the Los Angeles River from the zoo, and when the United States entered World War I and the city council banned the use

This page: One can see from these pictures that the old zoo lacked adequate cage space for the animals.

of beef for feeding animals, many cats died after being fed horse meat. It is believed that the horse meat may have been tainted. By the mid-1920s, the city, which had inadvertently helped cause some of the problems, all but stopped its funding of the zoo, and even though the Griffith Park Zoo was struggling, it took in more animals.

Even though the Los Angeles Zoo was in competition with the Selig/Jungle Zoo, there was a mutual respect and cooperation between the two entities. Selig had built the first successful Hollywood studio and subsequently built the zoo to house animals for his films. He donated animals to Griffith Park on occasion, and then, when Selig was forced to sell his studio and zoo, a few of the animals were sent to the Griffith Park Zoo; the rest stayed and became part of the new Luna Park Zoo in 1925. By 1932, Luna Park Zoo had become the California Zoological Gardens. Then, after severe flood damage and facing dwindling funds and attendance, the Zoopark, as it came to be called, closed its gates permanently. By this time, many of its animals were facing death from starvation, and a call went out to "all persons with civic consciousness and human liking for animals" to come to the creatures' aid. The sheriff's office was flooded with requests, but the Griffith Park Zoo was there to help, and many of the animals found a new home there.

In the mid-1930s, the Griffith Park Zoo got a huge boost when FDR's Works Progress Administration decided to add the zoo to its list. The work would go on for just over a year and provide new cages, paddocks and pens, and the WPA also provided $500,000 for new bear caves. But as we know, money can't solve all problems. Trying to get the bears into their new digs was a challenge in and of itself. The zoo superintendent, Byron Gibson, couldn't get the two bears to move into their new space. Every time he tried to move them, they would begin fighting with each other. One bear, Elsie, had to be coaxed to move with cold, high-pressure water, while the other, Alice, was fed raisin bread and sugar, not exactly a good diet for the animal. Then Rufus, the 625-pound lion, wound up in the deep moat of his cage and was stuck there all night until they could figure out how to safely remove him.

No matter how hard zookeepers tried, things kept getting worse, as did the publicity. Animals were getting into fights, including tortoises, polar bears, birds and other animals, and a baby zebra and a young bear were both found with broken necks after crashing into their fences. A leopard was even said to have "died of fright" after injuring his paw. All of this could have been avoided, but no one thought about space for the animals. Given the amount of work and money that had gone into the

The animals were kept so close together that different species, predator and prey, would fight through the bars of their cages.

new construction of the Griffith Park Zoo, the new facilities were woefully inadequate for the over one thousand animals the zoo had brought in over the years. In 1949, chief zookeeper Charles Allen went on a crusade for a bigger zoo. He stated, "The zoo is so cramped I am fearful my kangaroos, wallabies and antelopes will forget, for lack of space to practice, how to take a respectable leap."

By the 1950s, reports of feuds between zoo employees were rampant, with one leveling charges against his coworkers that they were putting sugar into his gas tank to ruin his car. There were reports of monkeys being mistreated and beaten by zookeepers, a deadly fight between polar bears that could have been stopped but wasn't and even penguins purposely being suffocated by chlorine gas. Many folks at the time believed that these reports may have been made up, or at the very least highly exaggerated, by LA councilwoman Rosalind Wyman. Wyman was on the board of the nonprofit organization Friends of the Zoo and was determined to see the Griffith Park Zoo shut down in favor of a new "Super Zoo" in Elysian Park. In a statement Wyman made in 1954, she called the Griffith Park Zoo "a mess. Perhaps the worst zoo for any city of 100,000 population or [more]"—an easy statement for a councilperson voting against funding for a zoo she wants to replace

The big cat enclosures were woefully inadequate for these majestic wild animals.

while having political and monetary aspirations to make. The Griffith Park Zoo's employees were calling for a larger facility, the animal population was growing and complaints were now coming from the zoo's visitors, who were seeing the overcrowded, aging facility and calling out their concern for the animals' well-being. With newspapers', guests' and employees' unwanted recognition of the Griffith Park Zoo's plight spreading nationwide, in 1958, voters approved an $8 million bond to be used to build a new zoo.

As usually happens when government red tape and politicians collide, political debates about where the new zoo would be built ensued, with each councilmember vying for their own district to win the bid. And even though the money from the bond was earmarked solely for the zoo, heated public debate over how the money would be spent reared its ugly head. All these debates, headline fodder as they were, were bad enough, but even the management of the new zoo was up for debate. After several years of embarrassing political theater, construction finally began on the new Los Angeles Zoo—only two miles down the road from the old Griffith Park Zoo and still within park boundaries. The Los Angeles Zoo and Botanical Gardens opened on December 6, 1966, with two thousand animals, many from the old Griffith Park Zoo, which had closed in August. After fifty years, the old zoo was gone, but many of the tortured animals are said to still reside there even today.

After the old zoo was shuttered, some of the cages and pens were demolished, but many remain to this day. Of those, some are still locked and off-limits, but others have been repurposed and made into picnic areas, as has the entire area that used to be the zoo. The place gives off a strange vibe during the day, an almost ominous feeling that there are eyes watching you from the darkened recesses of the cages surrounding your table. It is not uncommon to catch movement out of the corner of your eye, as if animals are still roaming their pens, but when one turns to look, nothing can be seen but an empty cage. As eerie as the old zoo is during the day, many say that when night falls, the area becomes more ominous and just downright scary. This is when the animals come out to play.

The old zoo has become a popular spot for ghost hunters and urban legend seekers to come and explore the unknown. Stories from these adventure seekers are plentiful and range from the mundane to the truly frightening. During the day, folks have heard whispered sounds that many believe come from the spirits of animals who were neglected. These reports usually describe the sounds as faint, but at night, they're said to be anything but. Ghost hunters have reported that while wandering around the old grounds,

Some enclosures have been turned into picnic areas. Many relaxing and having lunch at these tables have heard spectral animals prowling, growling and whimpering.

they have heard a distinct shuffling coming from inside the now-empty cages. Many say that it sounds as though an animal is moving about, as if it is still caged and looking for a way out of its confinement. These folks say that it is also common to hear growls coming from these same cages, as if a lion, tiger or other large cat is still present and confined. These reports have become so commonplace that it is getting hard to deny that these animals may still be present at the zoo.

Sounds are one thing, but seeing is another. Many folks coming to the old zoo after dark have reported seeing spectral animals both in and out of the cages. Many of the bars were removed from the pens and cages so picnic tables could be placed inside, and many wonder if the animals that are seen walking the grounds of the old zoo have been freed by this. Bears seem to be the most common sight reported, and these are generally seen near where their old caves would have been. These bears are said to simply wander around as if still among the living before vanishing from sight. One woman said she saw an elephant wandering around in front of some cages and that the beast turned its head toward her and extended its trunk as if expecting her to give it peanuts; this animal simply vanished when no food was offered. A more frightening tale comes from a group of kids who had gone up to the old zoo one night on a dare and swear they saw a "giant lion" come prancing out of one of the open cages. When the lion noticed them, it let out a loud roar, growled and lunged at them. The kids said that as they ran, they looked back and saw that the lion was chasing them and gaining ground, but as it got near, one of them let out a bloodcurdling scream and the lion gave one final roar and vanished from sight. The kids said they didn't wait around to see if it would reappear but kept running as fast as they could, got into their car and sped away, never to return.

As spectacular as these reports may seem, there are other, less dramatic reports that we hope are simply not true. The reason for my saying this is my love of animals. Folks, both those who visit during the day and those who venture into the old zoo at night, have reported hearing the sounds of animals in distress: cats hissing before whimpering in pain, growls followed by moans as anguish strikes them and the sounds of many other animals crying out in torment from whatever past lives they are reliving. So many reports of this type of activity have come from the old zoo that it gives one pause when it comes to investigating this area. Let us hope that these animals find peace over the rainbow bridge.

It is not only animal spirits that make themselves known in and near the old zoo. Doña Petronilla has been known to appear to folks who come to this spot. Petronilla, of course, is seen in many places in Griffith Park, and her specter being seen here has caused folks to think that it may be the curse she placed on the park that keeps the animals from passing on. Don Feliz is also known to show himself in the area, usually during severe lighting storms. This, again, is said to tie in with the curse of Petronilla. Many other spirits are said to wander this section of Griffith Park, and most folks believe these to be some of the many murder victims who have either been killed in the park's confines or who have had their bodies placed here after death. There are also many who simply had their ashes spread in the place they loved in life. Whatever the case may be, the old Griffith Park Zoo may be the most haunted place in the park, if not the city.

As humans, we have an obligation to be good stewards of our planet, and that does not stop at the environment, oceans and water but extends to all living things on Earth. We don't like to think of ourselves as part of the animal kingdom, but that is exactly what we are, each of us nothing more or less than one of the wondrous creatures living on this small planet. It is our job to protect those who cannot protect themselves and keep animals alive and well, not only for the benefit of future generations but also for the well-being of our world. Zoos, although many deride their existence, have a

The old zoo was finally shut down, and a new, more humane zoo took its place, two miles away.

job in protecting the astonishing variety of life Earth offers. Zoos have kept species from becoming extinct, they have bred others that would be gone without their aid and they study and teach us how to keep life thriving. I, for one, hope they keep giving back to Earth and all the life that lives here.

CHAPTER 13

THE LEGEND OF PICNIC TABLE 29

There are urban legends all over the world. Many spring from folktales that have been told and retold for generations on end, others have come from parents trying to cow their children into good behavior and others still are spread simply by teenagers' imaginations regarding local haunted houses and creatures that lurk in the woods after seeing a raccoon's glowing eyes in the firelight. Once the Internet came on the scene, a rebirth of urban legends began and spread, and now so many stories have come from creative minds that it is hard to tell truth from fiction. Some of these urban legends may have a bit of truth in the telling, most are simply works of the mind and some, like the legend of haunted picnic table no. 29, are so creepy in their simplicity that, even if not factual, they must be told and retold to keep the fun and fright going for future generations.

The story begins in 1976 on Halloween night when a young couple out for a walk in Griffith Park sat down at picnic table no. 29 for a rest. The young lovers kissed, which led to more kissing, which led to—well, we will leave some to the imagination. While lying atop the table, they heard a loud snapping coming from the tree that was growing next to the table and both looked up in time to see a giant branch break loose from the trunk and come crashing down. They did not, however, have time to get out of the way. The large, heavy tree limb fell on the couple, killing them—we hope—instantly. The young lovers said to be crushed to death that night, so we are told, were Nancy Jeanson, age twenty, and Rand Garrett, age twenty-two.

The parents of these high school sweethearts were, of course, devastated by the deaths of their children, and since the two had planned on getting married, the parents thought that cremating the couple and spreading their ashes over the last place they made love would be a fitting way for the couple to spend their afterlife together. The parents brought together their children's friends, walked up to picnic table no. 29, held a brief goodbye ceremony and then watched as the young lovers' ashes floated over and away from the table and into Griffith Park history, just two of many folks who have had their ashes spread on the grounds of the park.

Most folks would think this was the end of the tragic love story, but it was actually just the beginning. It seems that Nancy and Rand were not content with simply fading from memory or leaving the area where their mortal remains were cast to the winds and the earth. Since that fateful night in 1976, eerie things have occurred around table no. 29, many indicating that Rand and Nancy want to be left alone and certainly don't want the tree that did the deadly deed to be removed or the branch that killed them to be moved from the tabletop where they died.

The tales began only two months after the lovers' memorial, when, we are told, maintenance worker Morris Carl was tasked with removing the branch and the tree from around the picnic table so it could once again be used as it was meant to be: as a place to rest and eat for hikers in the area. According to Carl, he drove up to the picnic table a couple of days after receiving the order to remove the tree with every intention of completing the task—and, he said, he didn't figure on getting scared out of his wits while trying to do so. According to the supposedly now lost incident report he filed with his supervisor, he showed up just before noon and began sawing the branches from the top of the tree, in preparation for the crew that was going to meet him later with a stump grinder and branch chipper/shredder machines. Carl only managed to begin topping the tree before his chainsaw simply stopped working. He tried starting the machine but was unable, so he climbed down to inspect the chainsaw to see if he could figure out what was wrong with it. Unable to get the saw working, he went to his truck to get another one, but it, too, would not run. That is when he began to get a weird feeling.

Morris Carl, after failing to get his chainsaw working, decided to work on the lower branches with a handsaw. He said that while he'd been up in the tree with the power saw, as soon as he cut off the crown of the tree, a severe chill hit him, a cold that ran so deep he half expected it to start snowing. The extreme cold had lessened once he was back at his truck but had not

While not hard to find, the hike up to picnic table no. 29 is a steep climb up a dirt trail and an abandoned road.

completely gone away. Now, as he approached the tree with the smaller saw, the chill returned full force, and the nearer he came to the tree, the more intense the cold. This time, however, he began hearing a weird moaning and crying. He said that when he stopped approaching the tree to listen, the sound went away; then as he walked closer, the moaning and crying began once again. Carl said that the cold became so intense that he had to go back to his truck to put on his coat, and that is when all hell broke loose.

As Morris Carl opened the door to his truck, he began hearing an odd noise behind him, coming from the tree. As he turned to look, he said he saw the tree begin to shake: "The tree just went crazy. Not just lightly shaking but bouncing up and down as if someone was picking it up and dropping it." According to the story, parts of the tree landed on the table with so much force that it knocked all the tools that Carl had set on the table off and scattered them all over the ground. He said that as soon as all the tools were off the table, the shaking simply stopped, but all was certainly not quiet. Carl said that he heard the moaning once again coming from the area of the tree, but this time, it was accompanied by a voice coming from right beside him in the cab of the truck. The voice whispered into his ear, "Leave us alone." At this point, Carl tried to start the engine of the truck, but it wouldn't turn over. That is when he heard a squeaking coming from the inside of the windshield. He hadn't noticed that the glass had completely fogged over, but now he saw words appearing on the glass, "Next time you die." The truck finally started after the words appeared, and Morris Carl floored the gas and sped away, never to return to the area.

The following morning, Carl put in for a transfer out of Griffith Park, but not before letting his supervisor know what had happened and why he had left all the department's tools just lying on the ground in the public park. His supervisor, supposedly a man by the name of Dennis Higgs, was, as one can assume, not happy with his employee—but more than that, he could not stop making fun of Carl. No matter how many times Carl tried to tell Higgs that his tale was true, Higgs would only laugh. So angry was Carl that he made a bet with his supervisor that he couldn't go up to table no. 29 and complete the task. The bet was for $500, and Higgs himself, so sure that Carl was making up the whole story, said that not only would he finish the job, but he would also do it in the dead of night. This would be the last time Morris Carl would see Dennis Higgs alive.

The following morning, a jogger out for an early morning run along Mount Hollywood Drive discovered a city vehicle idling on the side of the road, its headlights on and its radio tuned to a music station. The truck was facing a picnic table, where a tree branch lay across the tabletop. The jogger couldn't see anyone about, so he decided to walk around and see if anyone was in the area. As the man walked past picnic table no. 29, he saw a pair of legs behind a bush and, on inspection, found a man lying on his back, eyes wide open, mouth set in a grimace and obviously dead. The jogger had found the dead body of Dennis Higgs. The jogger also found an idling chainsaw, its blade bent into a perfect U shape, with the saw blade still in its grove.

The coroner's report stated the cause of death was a massive heart attack. What they couldn't account for were the drag marks that indicated he had been dragged at least fifteen feet from where he died and why there had been no footprints or other indications of how he had been moved. It was also undetermined how the man's brown hair had gone completely white or why there seemed to be a look of pure horror frozen on his face. The paramedics and the coroner may not have known what happened, but Morris Carl was sure that his boss had been scared to death by the same spirits that had warned him to stay away only two days before Higgs's body was found.

This is not the only story that comes from the area of table no. 29. According to a tale told by a Griffith Park ranger, the man actually encountered the ghosts of Rand and Nancy in 2022. Of course, the ranger would only tell his tale on condition of anonymity. The story goes that at about ten o'clock at night, the ranger had just come off break, and while admiring the scenery along the Mulholland Trail, he passed the picnic table without realizing he was now on Mount Hollywood Drive. He said that as he slowly drove by the table, he heard what he described as an unearthly noise coming from somewhere in the brush next to table no. 29. He had never heard anything like it before or since. It began as a mournful sobbing that somehow morphed into a horrible scream, followed by a maniacal laugh. As the hair began to stand straight up on the back of his neck and arms, the sound began to change from a laugh to a scream and then alternated between the two. Thinking that someone might be in trouble, the ranger tried to radio for help, but all he could get on his two-way was static.

The ranger, unable to radio for help, said that all his training told him to stay in his vehicle, so switching on his truck's spotlight, he turned it toward the table and the eerie sound coming from behind it. As the light shone on the table and the tree next to it, he could see what looked to be two shrouded figures standing atop the table. As the light illuminated them, they froze, gazed at him with glowing red eyes and then dashed for the bushes and trees of Griffith Park and out of the spotlight.

All the ranger's training told him not to give chase, but—thinking that the two might need help and admitting that curiosity had gotten the better of him—he headed into the night after them. As he moved into the brush, the screaming suddenly stopped—just as he passed picnic table no. 29 and the fallen tree limb. At this point, he was overcome with a deep feeling of dread and, possibly, evil. There, in the now quiet of the night, the ranger knew that whatever it was he had seen was not happy at his being there and would do whatever was necessary to get rid of him. As the ranger debated what to do, his flashlight went dark, and the feeling of hatred toward him intensified.

In complete darkness and fear, the ranger turned and was about to run for his truck when he was suddenly held in a suffocating embrace. An icy cold breath washed across his neck, and it felt as if someone or something had grabbed him around the chest and was breathing on him. That is when he heard a soft but menacing voice whisper in his ear, "Leave us alone." Either from unbridled terror or what he later said was the smell of putrid death that washed over him, he passed out. When the ranger woke up, it was still dark out, and he noticed a burning pain on his chest. Looking down, he found that his shirt was unbuttoned, and scratched into his chest, surrounded by his own dried blood, were the words, "Next time you die." The ranger put in a transfer demand and never set foot in Griffith Park again.

Over the years, Griffith Park officials have repeatedly tried to clear the table, but every time an attempt is made, those sent to do the work have been deterred by unexplained tool malfunctions, strange shaking coming from the tree itself and supposed whispered threats that seem to emanate out of the air surrounding them. Today, all attempts to clear picnic table no. 29 have stopped. It is as if the powers that be at Griffith Park have surrendered to the young couple and figure they'll just let the sleeping dead lie.

You can still hike up to picnic table no. 29, but make sure you bring good boots and plenty of water, and also be aware that this spot has become popular with all sorts of different folks. From Wiccans who come to work various types of magic, believing the area to possibly have a lay line, to occult practitioners and those worshiping a deity that requires sacrifices,

The table where, it is said, the lovers were killed and their spirits threaten—and kill—to be left alone.

you may run into all sorts here. Of course, most of the people you'll come across are ordinary hikers and nature lovers just out for a nice day in a beautiful setting. From afar, the table and bench look ordinary, aside from the fallen tree branch, but as you move closer, you may begin to see—and, some say, feel—a difference. The table itself is now covered in gifts left by both those just paying their respects to Rand and Nancy and by paranormal enthusiasts, some left as "trigger" objects. There are crosses, flowers, dead flowers, cryptic messages, Wiccan peace symbols and graffiti. Scrawled across the broken tabletop are the etched words, "RIP Rand and Nancy." It is truly an odd sight sitting within the pristine surroundings of Griffith Park and could be a shock for those coming across the table who were not aware of its existence.

Whether the story of picnic table no. 29 is true or an urban legend or even a story that has now caused strange things to occur simply by existing is really no longer a matter for simple discussion. This lonely picnic table along a peaceful stretch of road and trail in an out-of-the-way area of Griffith Park is now firmly embedded in the legends and lore of the city of Los Angeles. It could no more be removed from the citizen's psyche or memory than a soul could be removed from its human. Most likely nothing more than an urban legend, it is one that will forever be an integral part of the heart of Los Angeles and one that is a fitting end to the story about the history and haunts of the paranormal heart of Los Angeles, Griffith Park.

CHAPTER 14
HAUNTABLE MENTION

There are so many haunted locations in the heart of Los Angeles that there is no way to write about them all in a single book. I have tried to share with my readers the most interesting and historic haunted places in the city, but there are a few others that I wanted to at least mention that deserve recognition, so I have included them, in brief, in this chapter.

LOS ANGELES CITY HALL

City hall in Los Angeles may be one of the most recognizable buildings in the world, not because folks know it as the seat of government for LA but because so many people around the world have seen it destroyed time and time again. Originally built in 1928, city hall was first destroyed in the 1953 film *War of the Worlds* (based on the novel by H.G. Wells). Since then, city hall has been destroyed by aliens at least four times, plus a few earthquakes, a giant dragon, tornadoes and even a volcano. Yes, Los Angeles City Hall is well known for not surviving any and all disasters. Though city hall has never really been destroyed, it is also known as one of the most haunted municipal buildings in California.

No one truly knows why the building is haunted; we can only speculate. Rumor has it that there was once a morgue in the building; however, it's

LA City Hall, the most "destroyed" municipal building in history.

most likely being confused with the morgue in the basement of the old Hall of Justice. Richard Carradine, founder of Ghost Hunters of Urban Los Angeles (GHOULA), once stated that when LA banned fortune-telling in the early 1900s, mystics protested and cursed city hall to forever host the lost souls of the city's dead. This could be the reason that the municipal building is haunted, or it could simply be that many folks have come to city hall for solutions to their problems only to be turned away by uncaring politicians, causing these same folks to walk the halls after death, still seeking answers. Whatever the reason, there are many stories about the specters of the building.

Security guards patrolling city hall at night have reported seeing shadows moving about the building, always from afar but easily in view. Many of the guards refuse to go to floors two, three, four, twenty-seven and twenty-eight after dark when everyone is gone. These are, according to the guards and many other employees, the most haunted floors of the building. It is not unusual to hear footsteps walking around on these floors, even though it is certain that everyone has gone home for the evening. The most pronounced of these footfalls are high heels that seem to walk at a quickened pace, as if the wearer is late for a meeting. Many of the guards say that you can actually feel someone walking beside you on these floors, even though no one can be seen.

Even the guards who refuse to go to these floors report seeing phantom figures flitting about on security cameras to the point that they must send someone to investigate to see if there is someone actually there. Of course, there is nary a soul once they arrive to check out the disturbance. Many believe that at least one of the spirits who haunts city hall is that of Councilman Gilbert Lindsey. Lindsey was the first Black council member in Los Angeles and had worked his way up from city hall janitor to becoming a distinguished member of the city council. Lindsey died at the ripe old age of ninety in December 1990. One might understand why the honorable councilman has remained in the halls of the building where he worked so hard for justice.

It seems fitting that a place that has been destroyed so many times should now be haunted by so many folks that have lived and worked in the City of Angels—or is it simply cinematic retribution?

CLIFTON'S CAFETERIA

High school cafeterias: I imagine most of us remember them from our school days and remember them fondly… Well, OK, not many but a very few. As bad as the food was in school, there is a place in downtown LA that not only has decent cafeteria food but also an atmosphere like one of those burger places in Disneyland along the Rivers of America: woodsy, cozy and full of stuffed animals. Clifton's Cafeteria is one of the most unusual eateries in the state and, just like Disneyland, has its fair share of ghosts.

Clifford Clinton was a devout Christian who had been in the cafeteria business for a while in San Francisco when he gave up his ownership of what had once been his father's restaurant and moved to Los Angeles in 1931. With the Depression raging, Clinton opened up a cafeteria, but if someone couldn't pay, he gave them their meal for free. On the wall inside the cafeteria was a sign that read, "Pay what you wish." Over time, this policy had to be changed to keep the place from going out of business, but Clifton's Cafeteria never let anyone go hungry. Even today, although it's no longer owned by the Clinton family, the new owners have kept the Clifton's new, old sign that simply says, "Dine free unless delighted." Who wouldn't love a restaurant with that kind of commitment?

As for the ghosts that haunt this wonderful establishment, many folks have been seeing them for years; however, it was during the recent renovations that they have become more well known than ever before. Workers began seeing the "Blonde Woman" appearing in photos and videos almost from the first day work began. One restoration worker, taking pictures of an area to be worked on, saw what appeared to be a woman's face in one photo. After enlarging the picture, he could clearly see a woman, who hadn't been there at the time the photo was taken, staring back at him. In speaking with other workers, he found out that many of them knew about this phantom and that she had shown up in a lot of the video footage security had recorded. Most believe that this is the spirit of Terri Richmond, Clifford Clinton's mistress. The woman died in 2010, and her children, wanting to reunite their mother with the love of her life, spread her ashes within Clifton's Cafeteria hoping that Clifford was there as well.

Another possibility is that the woman may be Clifford's daughter, Jean Clinton Roeschlaub. Jean Clinton was found murdered in her home on August 2, 2006. Clinton was discovered face down in her sixteenth-floor penthouse, and the police said "suspicious circumstances" surrounded the scene. The case has never been solved. As with many unsolved murders,

Clifton's Brookdale cafeteria: history, good food and ghosts.

it is possible that Clifford's daughter may not be at rest and has decided to return to the place her father built and that she helped run for decades after his death. Of course, it could also be both women who haunt the cafeteria. Other things that have been reported at Clifton's include ladders that move on their own, orbs that flit around and can be seen with the naked eye and shadows that dart about just at the periphery of one's vision.

Philippe the Original

Who doesn't love a roast beef sandwich dripping with juices that flavor the French bread with succulent gravy? That is exactly what you get when you step into the Philippe the Original sandwich shop, home of the original French dip sandwich. Although two competing delis claim to be the inventors of the iconic dripping delight, Philippe the Original and Cole's Delicatessen, only Philippe Mathieu, a transplanted Frenchman, seems to have a plausible reason for the claim. At the turn of the 1900s, one of the popular fashions for ladies was called the French dip dress, and as Mathieu claimed that his invention was purely accidental, it would make sense that a Frenchman would name his creation after something decidedly French and famous. Cole's, on the other hand, didn't start claiming it had created the sandwich until ten years after Philippe had already staked its claim, and as there is no one and nothing remotely French about Cole's, it seems odd that Cole's would call it a French dip. Regardless, the battle is ongoing, which makes things that much better for diners, as both sandwiches are still delicious. One thing Philippe the Original has that Cole's may not, however, is a host of ghosts.

It is said that before Philippe the Original took over the building, the upper floor was a brothel, although the restaurant says it was "a machine shop with a hotel on the second floor." This "hotel," so it is said, is at the heart of the hauntings at Philippe's. Many of the restaurant's employees dislike having to go up to the second floor, which now has seating for the restaurant. Those cleaning the tables and the eating area have reported being pushed and touched even though no one other than the employee is in the upper area, and the strong smell of perfume is often noticed, sometimes so strong that it becomes overpowering. One employee actually said that they saw a woman in a red dress walking around the upstairs area who passed right through tables as if they weren't there, while a longtime customer reported seeing a "strange-looking" woman in a purple dress sitting at a table in the main floor dining room area.

Philippe the Original, birthplace of the French Dip sandwich, served with spirits.

Ghost Hunters of Urban Los Angeles (GHOULA) may have an answer to who this woman may be. In 2008, GHOULA held an investigation meetup at Philippe the Original and discovered through a tarot reading that the woman in question is not one of the "working girls" from the brothel but the madam who ran the "hotel." The medium performing the divination said that the madam was pacing the hallways still looking for money that had been hidden from her in the building or protecting her stash of cash. GHOULA investigators said the dowsing rods they were using began spinning "like helicopter blades," and so many orbs were caught that it looked like a light show. One of the members who was there at the time even sketched a drawing of what he believed the spirt lady looked like.

From lights that turn on and off after the restaurant has closed and employees are trying to clean up to chairs and other small items that move around on their own, Philippe the Original serves not only the best historic dipped sandwiches in downtown Los Angeles but also a fun and spooky helping of ghosts.

EPILOGUE

Los Angeles is known as the home of Hollywood, the Dodgers, Venice Beach, bikinis and the famous Watts Towers sculpture. It is a place folks from around the world visit, some to become movie stars in their own right and others simply to stargaze and ogle their favorite movie idols. Few come here to discover the spiritual side of this urban sprawl or to investigate the many haunted locations both in and around the city. However, for those in the know, Los Angeles and environs is perhaps one of the most haunted cities in the country, if not the world.

As seen on many paranormal TV shows, Heritage Square Museum in Los Angeles has many historical and haunted Los Angeles homes for the ParaTraveler to explore.

What I have touched on in this simple tome barely scratches the surface of the haunted locations in downtown Los Angeles, let alone the entire city; to do them justice would take more than ten books, and large ones at that. I hope you've found this sample of haunted locations in LA both enjoyable and educational and that it inspires you to look for opportunities to seek out the myriad spirits that reside within the City of Angels.

Bibliography

Griffith Park

Bartlett, James, and Mary Forgione. "Our Guide to Griffith Park: How to Safely Explore Its Wild, Classic and Hidden Gems." *LA Times*, September 4, 2020. https://www.latimes.com/lifestyle/story/2020-09-04/beginner-guide-griffith-park.

Bates, Norm. "Legend of the Haunted Griffith Park Picnic Table." *LA Times*, October 30, 2006.

California Curiosities. "Haunted Picnic Table 29: Chasing Horny Ghosts and Urban Legends in Griffith Park." http://www.californiacuriosities.com/haunted-picnic-table-29.

Friends of Griffith Park. "Griffith Park Zoo—The Great World Zoo That Never Was (1912–1966)." July 9, 2019. https://friendsofgriffithpark.org/griffith-park-zoo-the-great-world-zoo-that-never-was-1912-1966.

The Hollywood Sign. "Explore the History of the Sign." https://www.hollywoodsign.org/history.

Meares, Hadley. "The Complex Life of Griffith J. Griffith." PBS SoCal, October 16, 2019. https://www.kcet.org/shows/lost-la/the-complex-life-of-griffith-j-griffith.

———. "A Whimpering Roar: The Old Griffith Park Zoo, Then and Now." PBS SoCal, April 13. 2015. https://www.pbssocal.org/history-society/a-whimpering-roar-the-old-griffith-park-zoo-then-and-now.

Rylah, Juliet Bennett. "Griffith Park Turns 120 This Year: Here's Why It's LA's Most Important Park." Thrillist, 2017. January 7, 2017. https://www.thrillist.com/lifestyle/los-angeles/griffith-park-observatory-los-angeles-history-anniversary.

Smith, Nathan. "The Hidden History of the Hollywood Sign." *Smithsonian Magazine*, July 13, 2023. https://www.smithsonianmag.com/history/the-hidden-history-of-the-hollywood-sign-180982518.

Vintage Los Angeles. "Los Angeles Myths: The Cursed Ranch; Griffith Park." https://vintagelosangeles.org/griffithpark.

Olvera Street

Creason, Glen. "The Colorful Rebirth of Olvera Street in 1930 L.A." *Los Angeles Magazine*, May 15, 2018. https://lamag.com/lahistory/citydig-the-colorful-rebirth-of-olvera-street-in-1930-la.

Mears, Hadley. "Looking Back at Christine Sterling, the Maternalistic, Problematic 'Mother of Olvera Street.'" *LA Weekly*, July 11, 2017. https://www.laweekly.com/looking-back-at-christine-sterling-the-maternalistic-problematic-mother-of-olvera-street.

Trausch, John D. "History." Olvera-Street.com. https://www.olvera-street.com/history.

Wallace, Kelly. "Forgotten Los Angeles History: The Chinese Massacre of 1871." Los Angeles Public Library, Friday, May 19, 2017. https://www.lapl.org/collections-resources/blogs/lapl/chinese-massacre-1871.

Avila Adobe

"The Avila Adobe: LA's Oldest Haunted House?" https://cryptic79.rssing.com/chan-15693651/article31.html?zx=814.

Holm, Max. "The Avila Adobe Still Stands After Nearly 200 Years." December 9, 2015. https://www.uscannenbergmedia.com/2015/12/09/the-avila-adobe-still-stands-after-nearly-200-years.

SAH Archipedia. "Avila Adobe." https://sah-archipedia.org/buildings/CA-01-037-0002.

Pico House

Halfhill, Layla. "Pico House—Ghosts of Old Los Angeles." Scare Pop, September 3, 2010. https://scarepop.com/2010/09/03/pico-house-ghosts-of-los-angeles.

Harvey, Steve. "Masonic Hall's History Quieter Than the Fraternity's Folklore." October 11, 2009. https://www.latimes.com/archives/la-xpm-2009-oct-11-me-then11-story.html.

Kiddle. "Merced Theatre (Los Angeles, California) Facts for Kids." https://kids.kiddle.co/Merced_Theatre_(Los_Angeles,_California).

Pacific Coast Architecture Database. "Merced Theatre, Downtown, Los Angeles, CA." https://pcad.lib.washington.edu/building/1519.

Pio Pico State Historic Park. "History of Pico Pico's 'El Ranchito.'" http://piopico.org/History_of_Pio_Pico_El_Ranchito.htm.

Spitzzeri, Paul R. "Through the Viewfinder: The Pico House, Merced Theater, and Masonic Lodge, Los Angeles, ca. 1876–1880." *Homestead Blog*, October 11, 2017. https://homesteadmuseum.blog/2017/10/11/through-the-viewfinder-the-pico-house-merced-theater-and-masonic-lodge-los-angeles-ca-1876-1880.

Union Station

Burns, Adam. "Los Angeles Union Station: Interior, History, Amtrak." American-Rails.com. Last revised March 7, 2024. https://www.american-rails.com/laupt.html.

Flannery, Pat. "Remembering the 1931 'Trunk Murderess' Case." azcentral, June 21, 2016. https://www.azcentral.com/story/news/local/phoenix-history/2016/06/21/remembering-1931-trunk-murderess-case/86143794.

Geier, Max G. "Conviction of Robert Folkes." Oregon Encyclopedia. https://www.oregonencyclopedia.org/articles/conviction-of-robert-folkes.

Ghost Hunters of Urban Los Angeles (blog). "Highlights from Feb 2009 Spirits with Spirits at Union Station." February 15, 2009. http://ghoula.blogspot.com/2009/02/highlights-from-feb-2009-spirits-with.html.

The Great American Stations. "Los Angeles, CA—Union Station (LAX)." http://www.greatamericanstations.com/stations/los-angeles-ca-lax.

Murderpedia. "Robert E. Lee Folkes." https://murderpedia.org/male.F/f/folkes-robert.htm.

Phantom Los Angeles (blog). "Los Angeles Union Station." Thursday, September 27, 2012. http://phantomlosangeles.blogspot.com/2012/09/los-angeles-union-station.html.

Union Station Los Angeles. "History." https://unionstationla.com/history.

Dodger Stadium

Haunted Places. "Dodger Stadium." https://www.hauntedplaces.org/item/dodger-stadium.

Middleton, Sherri. "Haunted Sports Stadiums, Fields and Eerie Stories." October 23, 2017. https://sportseventsmediagroup.com/haunted-sports-stadiums.

Shatkin, Elina. "The Ugly, Violent Clearing of Chavez Ravine Before It Was Home to the Dodgers." May 1, 2023. https://laist.com/news/la-history/dodger-stadium-chavez-ravine-battle.

UCLA Library Digital Collections. "'Public Purpose' and Private Gain in the Chavez Ravine." Thursday, February 4, 2021. https://uclalibrary.github.io/lahousing/exhibits/chavezravine.

Hotel Cecil

Kranc, Lauren. "The Former Cecil Hotel Manager: 'I Believe in Ghosts... But I Don't Think They Run the Show Over There.'" February 10, 2021. https://www.esquire.com/entertainment/tv/a35463537/cecil-hotel-manager-amy-price-elisa-lam-interview.

Los Angeles City Planning. *Hotel Cecil*. https://planning.lacity.gov/StaffRpt/CHC/2016/12-15-2016/7_HotelCecil_Final.pdf.

Montalti, Victoria. "The Infamous Cecil Hotel, Where at Least 16 People Have Died, Recently Reopened—Here's Its History and What It's Like Today." Business Insider, March 9, 2022. https://www.businessinsider.com/cecil-hotel-history-what-its-like-today-photos-2022-3.

Hauntable Mention

Elliott, Farley. "Someone Finally Got to the Bottom of LA's Great French Dip Debate." Eater Los Angeles, March 28, 2016. https://la.eater.com/2016/3/28/11320334/who-invented-french-dip-sandwich-philippes-coles.

The Journalist. "Haunted LA: Gourmet Ghosts in the City of Angels." October 3, 2019. https://journalhotels.com/thejournalist/7451/haunted-la-gourmet-ghosts-in-the-city-of-angels.

Marshall, Colin. "Los Angeles in Buildings: City Hall." October 18, 2017. https://www.pbssocal.org/shows/lost-la/los-angeles-in-buildings-city-hall.
Philippe the Original. "Our History." https://www.philippes.com/about-us.
Silva, Valentina. "A (Harmless) Ghost May Be Roaming Clifton's Cafeteria." *Los Angeles Magazine*, October 29, 2015. https://lamag.com/dining/hungry-for-terror-l-a-s-haunted-restaurants-and-bars.
Weird California. "Clifton's Cafeteria." http://www.weirdca.com/location.php?location=291#google_vignette.

About the Author

Brian Clune is the cofounder of and the historian for Planet Paranormal Radio and Planet Paranormal Investigations. He has traveled the entire state of California researching its haunted hot spots and historical locations in an effort to bring knowledge of the paranormal and the wonderful history of the state to those interested in learning.

His interest in history has led him to volunteer aboard the USS *Iowa* and at the Fort MacArthur Military Museum, as well as giving lectures at colleges and universities around the state. He has been involved with numerous TV shows, including *Ghost Adventures*, *My Ghost Story*, *Dead Files* and *Ghost Hunters* and was the subject of a companion documentary for the movie *Paranormal Asylum*. He has also appeared on numerous local, national and international radio programs. Clune was the cohost of the radio program *The Full Spectrum Project*, which delved into subjects ranging from ghosts and murders to all things odd and weird, both natural and supernatural.

His other books include *California's Historic Haunts*, published by Schiffer Books, and the highly acclaimed *Ghosts of the Queen Mary*, published by The History Press, as well as *Ghosts and Legends of Alcatraz* and *Ghosts and Legends of Calico*, all with coauthor Bob Davis. Brian and Bob also teamed up to write the riveting biography of Ghost Box creator Frank Sumption. Clune is also the author of *Haunted San Pedro* and *Hollywood Obscura*, a spellbinding book dealing with Hollywood's dark and sordid tales of murder and ghosts. Clune is currently working on other titles for The History Press and is teaching courses in paranormal studies at California State University, Dominguez Hills.

Clune lives in Southern California with his loving wife, Terri; his three wonderful children; and, of course, Wandering Wyatt!

Other Books by Brian Clune

Ghosts of the Queen Mary (The History Press, 2014)

California's Historic Haunts (Schiffer Books, 2015)

Haunted San Pedro (The History Press, 2016)

Hollywood Obscura: Death, Murder and the Paranormal Aftermath (Schiffer Books, 2017)

Haunted Universal Studios (The History Press, 2018)

Ghosts and Legends of Alcatraz (The History Press, 2019)

Thinking Outside the Box: Frank Sumption, Creator of the Ghost Box (Palmetto Publishing, 2019)

Ghosts and Legends of Calico (The History Press, 2020)

Haunted Heart of San Diego (The History Press, 2021)

California's Haunted Route 66 (The History Press, 2022)

Dark Tourism: California (Schiffer Books, 2022)

Haunted Southern California (The History Press, 2022)

Legends and Lore Along California's Highway 395 (The History Press, 2022)

Ghosts and Legends of Hollywood (The History Press, 2023)

Brian Clune and his book *Ghosts of the Queen Mary* were featured in *LIFE: World's Most Haunted Places: Creepy, Ghostly and Notorious Spots* (2016).